KIM IL SUNG

For the Independent Peaceful Reunification of Korea

REVISED EDITION

Guardian Associates, Inc.
New York, N.Y.

$3.00

Printed in the United States of America

Library of Congress Cataloging in Publication Data

Kim, Il Sung, 1912-
For the independent, peaceful reunification of Korea.

Selections from the author's writings, speeches and reports, 1960-1976
Library of Congress catalogue number 76-25395

ISBN 0-917654-03-X (pbk.)
ISBN 0-917654-04-8

 159

ᴼForeword

For thousands of years, the Korean people lived and worked diligently in the same land with a shared language, culture and customs. Today, Korea is split in half, with the repressive regime of the southern zone oppressing its own people and threatening those of the north. How did this come about?

The tragedy of this national split began in September 1945 with the U.S. occupation of the south of the Korean peninsula at the end of World War 2. Upon landing in south Korea, the U.S. army established a "military administration" in order to hamper Korea from developing into a united, democratic independent state. The U.S. seized the real power in all fields of politics, economy, culture and military affairs in south Korea and reduced it to a colony and military base.

The U.S. occupation of south Korea and the ensuing partition of Korea have caused untold national sufferings and misfortunes to the entire Korean people. Washington has provoked one brutal war (1950-53), bringing the fratricidal conflagration to the Korean people, and is stepping up preparations for another war.

Korea remains divided for over 30 years now. The differences between the north and the south are growing in all fields and the community of the nation formed over a long historical period is gradually fading away. The abundant resources of the country and the creative talents of the people are not utilized in a coordinated way and many parents, wives, children, relatives and friends are living separated from each other.

The greatest and most urgent national task now facing the entire Korean people is to reunify the divided country. To this end, the great leader of the Korean people, President Kim Il Sung of the Democratic People's Republic of Korea (DPRK) has worked heart and soul for decades. In the process he has advanced principled and realistic proposals for reunification based upon the independent stand of the Korean people. President Kim Il Sung has said: "We have consistently maintained that

v

Korea's reunification should be achieved independently and peacefully on democratic principles without any interference from outside forces."

This basic line of national reunification laid down by President Kim Il Sung reflects the ardent aspirations of the entire Korean people for the country's reunification and the unanimous desire of the progressive people of the world and enjoys their support.

The DPRK government put forward proposals for national salvation on more than 130 occasions: they included the proposal for achieving reunification through a north-south general election; the proposal for realizing reunification by a gradual method through the institution of a north-south confederation as a transitional measure; the proposal for reducing the armies; for economic and cultural interchange; and the humanitarian proposal for mutual visits of people and the exchange of correspondence.

Several years ago, the DPRK government took the initiative in organizing a dialogue between the north and south, resulting in July 1972 in an historic North-South Joint Statement with independence, peaceful reunification and great national unity set forth by President Kim Il Sung as its keynote.

The DPRK then advanced concrete proposals to put the agreement into effect. On June 23, 1973, President Kim Il Sung advanced a five-point proposition of national reunification whose content was to remove military confrontation and ease tension between the north and the south; enhance cooperation and interchange between the north and the south; convene a Great National Congress composed of representatives of people of all strata and political parties and social organizations in the north and the south; institute a north-south confederation under the single name of the Confederal Republic of Koryo and enter the UN under the single name of the Confederal Republic of Koryo.

In spite of all these sincere efforts of the DPRK government and the ardent aspirations of the Korean people, none of these proposals has produced reunification due to the maneuvers of U.S. imperialism and its puppets in south Korea.

Due to the propaganda fed them by their government, the average American is completely ignorant of the true facts in Korea. Publication of this selection of some of the works of President Kim Il Sung on reunification is intended to help the American people become aware of the criminal role of the U.S. played in Korea, hopefully stimulating them to take action to force the Washington government to withdraw its 40,000 troops and nuclear weapons and stop the financial and political aid to the south Korean puppet regime.

Contents

CONTENTS

CONTENTS

Speech at the 15th Anniversary Celebration of the August 15 Liberation, the National Holiday of the Korean People [Excerpt]

August 14, 1960

Comrades, the building of socialism and the happy life of the people in the northern half of the Republic are exerting a tremendous revolutionary influence on the people in south Korea and immensely encouraging and inspiring them in their struggle against the U.S. imperialists and their lackeys.

The aggressive policy of the U.S. imperialists and the reactionary rule of the Syngman Rhee clique have reduced south Korea to a complete colony of the United States and a military base for launching another war. Fifteen years' occupation of south Korea by the U.S. imperialists since liberation has ruined south Korea's economy and driven its people into the mire of hunger and poverty.

The broad masses of the people in south Korea could no longer tolerate all the social evils and the appalling difficulty of living that results from U.S. colonial rule, and at last they rose in the heroic resistance struggle against the oppressors.

The mass uprising of the people which broke out throughout

1

south Korea this spring was the explosion of the long pent-up grievancès and resentment of south Korean people against U.S. imperialism and the Syngman Rhee clique. It was a just struggle demanding freedom and liberation, a new government and a new life.

In defiance of the armed suppression by the enemy, the broad sections of the people, including the youth, students and intellectuals, in south Korea fought heroically and overthrew the Syngman Rhee puppet government. This is the initial, great victory gained by the south Korean people in their struggle against the U.S. imperialists and their lackeys. Through their valiant struggle, they demonstrated the revolutionary mettle of the Korean people and, at the same time, gained precious experience and lessons.

The uprising of the south Korean people has shown that no amount of threat of the bayonet or deceptive tricks can enslave the people long or check their revolutionary struggle. The uprising has also shown that when the people are united and rise in the struggle against the oppressors, they can smash any stronghold of the imperialists, and that they can triumph only by mass struggle.

However, the recent struggle of the south Korean people was not carried on to the last, to a complete victory. This was because the broad masses of workers and peasants failed to take part in the struggle. Thus, the south Korean people have not yet won liberty and democracy, and their demands have not yet been realized.

For the south Korean people to win complete victory of democracy the broad masses of workers, peasants and other people should join in the struggle, which must be thoroughly anti-imperialist and anti-feudal.

So long as an aggressive army of foreign imperialism exists in his territory, no one can speak of his national independence nor can the people live in peace. At present, the root cause of our country's division and of all misery and sufferings of the south Korean people lies in the occupation of south Korea by the aggressive army of the U.S. imperialists and their aggressive policy. As long as south Korea is in the grip of that army, the peaceful reunification of our country will never be realized, nor will the south Korean people be free from the present miserable plight.

The U.S. imperialist aggressor army which is occupying south Korea is the ringleader of the reactionary forces there. It is a band of robbers plundering the south Korean people of their properties and perpetrating all sorts of atrocities. This imperialist aggressor army of the United States, the ringleader of reaction and gangsterism, is the primary target in the struggle of the south Korean people.

Therefore, the workers, peasants and all other sections of the population of south Korea must, first of all, resolutely oppose the U.S. imperialist aggressive forces and fight to force their army out of south Korea. When all the patriotic people in south Korea rise as one in the anti-U.S. struggle, these aggressors will be unable to stay there but will be compelled to withdraw.

The anti-imperialist struggle of the south Korean people must be linked with the anti-feudal struggle. In implementing their aggressive policy, the U.S. imperialists use and actively protect feudal landlords, comprador capitalists and reactionary bureaucrats in south Korea. The feudal landlords and comprador capitalists on their part serve to extend the influence of the aggressive forces of U.S. imperialism in south Korea and, in collusion with them, are oppressing and exploiting the people. Without fighting the feudal forces, therefore, the anti-imperialist struggle cannot be waged successfully, nor can the anti-feudal struggle be successful without fighting the aggressive imperialist forces.

Only when all the patriotic forces—the workers, peasants, youth, students, intellectuals, entrepreneurs, traders, etc.—are united as one man and launch a decisive struggle against the aggressive forces of U.S. imperialism and the feudal forces, can the south Korean people attain real freedom and liberation and win complete victory of democracy.

For the development of all patriotic and democratic movements in south Korea, full democracy should be ensured, above all, in political life. In a society where the people's free will is overridden and fascist oppression and terror are rampant, only corruption and degeneration will prevail and there can be no progress at all.

In south Korea today, the questions of the country's peaceful reunification and north-south negotiations are a topic of discussion.

However, certain reactionary circles in south Korea are scheming to resume suppression against the trend. The reactionary attempt to restore the same rule of fascist terror as that of the Syngman Rhee clique and destroy even the rudimentary gains made by the people at the cost of their precious blood must be smashed.

The south Korean people still have no elementary democratic rights and liberties. There is no freedom of speech, press, association, assembly or religion, and all progressive ideas and patriotic movements are suppressed. Especially communist ideology is still under a ruthless suppression.

If it is free to believe in Jesus Christ, why should it not be free to choose communist ideology?

Communist ideology is the most scientific and most progressive of all ideologies. One thousand million people in the world have already won freedom and liberation under the banner of communism and are enjoying a happy life. Communist ideology is gripping the hearts of increasing numbers of people on the globe; it is a banner of liberation and victory for them. In the northern half of the Republic communist ideology has become the dominant one, and the people have built a new, free and happy life under the banner of this ideology. Why then should it be banned and suppressed in south Korea?

Historical experience has proven that communist ideology is winning one victory after another and those who suppress it are bound to perish.

Needless to say, it is free for any individual to accept communist ideology or reject it. No one does or can force it upon others. But no ideas should ever be suppressed.

Everyone should be guaranteed the right and liberty to choose whatever ideology he likes, to express his views, and to propagate his ideals.

Moreover, freedom of association and assembly and a complete freedom of activities of every political party and social organization should be ensured. In south Korea at present there is no political party which represents the workers and peasants who comprise the vast majority of the population. Neither the Liberal Party nor the Democratic Party in south Korea is a workers' or peasants' party and neither of them can represent the interests of the working people. Workers and peasants must have their own political party which can represent their will and can fight for their interests. Such a political party must also have a legal status.

In north Korea, since right after liberation, the Democratic Party, a political party of the propertied classes, has been enjoying a legal status and freedom of activity. Why should the political party of the laboring people be banned in south Korea? It is another question which class has its political party in power, but the workers and peasants should also be able legally to organize a political party of their own, and this party too should have complete freedom of activity. Denying this is nothing but ignoring the will of the broadest masses of the working people and stifling their interests.

Only when freedom of expression is provided to every class and section of the population, particularly to the broad masses of the workers and peasants, and only when a complete freedom of activity is guaranteed to all political parties and social organizations including the party of the working people, will south Korean society be able to make progress and its people successfully carry out their struggle for national and social emancipation.

Today the U.S. imperialists, dismayed at the awakening of the south Korean people and their unceasing struggle, are resorting to every trick to maintain their colonial rule over south Korea. They are bringing new-type weapons into south Korea, reinforcing their troops there and intensifying war preparations, while frantically trying to put the paralysed puppet ruling apparatus in order. The south Korean reactionary clique is trying to dampen the fighting spirit of the people by means of repression and deception, faithfully carrying out the orders of their American masters.

The recent "elections to the National Assembly" held in south Korea are a glaring manifestation of such machinations of the U.S. imperialists and their stooges. The south Korean ruling circles are very noisy about the "elections," describing them as "most fair." In fact, however, these "elections" were also a fraud, effected with money, deception and terror, like all the previous "elections" held in south Korea. Everywhere south Korean people destroyed polling stations and ballot boxes, assaulted police stations and other puppet government organs, declared the elections null and void and held demonstrations. Through these mass struggles they laid bare the true nature of the so-called fair elections. The present "National Assembly," too, like that under Syngman Rhee's rule, has not a single representative of the workers and peasants.

Needless to say, such a "National Assembly" cannot be a representative organ of the people.

The south Korean rulers are prating as if the "new National Assembly" and the "new government" could practice democracy, rehabilitate the economy and stabilize the people's living. But this is no more than a trick to deceive the people.

South Korea has now been ruined irreparably in all fields of politics, economy and culture.

The U.S. imperialists' policy of ruthless colonial plunder and militarization has totally devastated the economy of south Korea.

South Korea has turned into a market for U.S. goods, and its industries are being ruined under the pressure of U.S. monopoly capital and the handful of comprador capital. The number of factories has been reduced to half compared with that in the years of Japanese imperialist rule, and most of the remaining medium and small enterprises have stopped or curtailed operation because of raw material shortage, lack of funds and markets, and heavy tax burdens. Agriculture, which holds an overwhelming proportion in south Korea's economy, has been extremely devastated. As compared with the closing years of Japanese imperialist rule, the sown area has been reduced by 600,000 *chongbo* and the grain output decreased by more than six million *sok.* Every year south Korea suffers from an acute food crisis, and it has become an area of chronic famine.

Today the south Korean people are in an indescribably wretched plight. The wages of the workers are less than one-third of the minimum living costs, and even their payment is usually overdue a few months, sometimes more than half a year. Peasants are cruelly exploited by landlords and usurers. Most of them are under heavy debts, and over one million peasant households run out of food every year. Millions of unemployed and semi-employed are on the verge of starvation, and hundreds of thousands of children are wandering around and begging in the streets.

How can the south Korean rulers cope with this situation and meet the demands of the people? How can they rehabilitate the bankrupt national industry and rural economy, give jobs to the millions of unemployed, and save the broad masses of the people from hunger and poverty?

So long as the U.S. imperialists keep occupying south Korea and our country remains divided, no one, however he may come into power, can save the ruinous situation in south Korea and meet the demands of the people. Nothing will change and, if anything, the Syngman Rhee government would be renamed, say as Syngman Chang government. But their status and fate would be the same. Nor would there be any improvement in the people's life. This has been fully proved by the experience of the past 15 years since liberation.

The south Korean people demanded liberty and the right to live and, above all, the solution of the burning problems of living. Unless these fundamental problems are settled, the struggle of the people will go on and gain in scope and strength.

No amount of repression and trickery by the U.S. imperialists and their stooges can put out the flames of the struggle now raging in south Korea, or keep them from growing fiercer.

On the occasion of the 15th anniversary of the August 15 Liberation, I, on behalf of the Workers' Party of Korea and the Government of the Republic, extend militant greetings to the south Korean people who are heroically fighting against the

U.S. imperialists and their lackeys, and convey to them the warm support and encouragement from the people in the northern half.

Comrades, the only way to save the present situation in south Korea and finally solve the Korean question lies in driving out the U.S. army and reunifying the country peacefully.

The peaceful reunification of our country must be achieved independently by holding free general elections throughout north and south Korea on a democratic basis without any foreign interference. This is our consistent stand on the question of national reunification.

The proposal of our Party and the Government of the Republic on the question of peaceful national reunification reflects the unanimous desire and interests of the entire Korean people and, accordingly, enjoys their unreserved support and approval. The bankruptcy of Syngman Rhee's clamors for "march north," and the ever-growing demand of the people for peaceful reunification in south Korea, conclusively testify to the correctness and vitality of our proposal for reunification.

The south Korean rulers are now compelled by the pressure of the people to speak of peaceful reunification. But they are only paying lip service to it; in reality they keep obstructing it.

Claiming that the "elections should be held only in north Korea," or that the "elections should be held under the UN supervision," they refuse to hold free, democratic elections.

Because Syngman Rhee wanted to maintain his one-man despotism at the expense of national interests, he was afraid of free north-south elections more than anything else. But why should one be afraid of the free elections if one truly stands for national independence and the interests of the people?

Why can't we Koreans solve the Korean question by ourselves? Why should foreigners meddle in this matter? This is an unbearable insult to our nation and it is designed to keep our people forever in the bondage of foreign imperialism.

The Korean people have a long history of thousands of years and time-honored cultural traditions. Today they have built a fine, new society by their own hands on half their territory and turned out as one for a complete liberation and prosperity of their country; they are a nation courageous, hardworking, resourceful, patriotic and strong in their sense of unity. Our people are capable of independently and admirably deciding their destinies without any others' interference.

The south Korean rulers say that they cannot accept a free north-south general election because it means "collaboration with the Communists" and involves the danger of being "communized."

However, those who really want to fight for the people and defend the interests of the nation will never be afraid of the Communists or oppose "collaboration with the Communists," because the Communists always work for the people; they are the most ardent defender of the national interests and the staunchest patriots. This was why the Japanese imperialists feared the Korean Communists more than anybody else and repressed them most ruthlessly.

Who was it but the Korean Communists that courageously fought against the Japanese imperialists, with fidelity to the revolution and the nation to the last moment, undaunted in the enemy's prisons or on the gallows? Who was it but the Korean Communists that, undergoing indescribable tribulations in the darkest period of Japanese imperialist rule, put up the 15-year-long bloody struggle with arms in their hands solely for the freedom and independence of the country?

Following liberation, the people in the northern half, under the leadership of the Communists, have firmly seized their destinies in their hands, upheld the independence and honor of their country and built a new, happy life. If communism was something bad, how in the north could the national economy develop so rapidly, towns and villages be built so beautifully as never before, the people's living standards improve daily and the national culture blossom so splendidly?

In the north there are a million members of the Workers' Party, the people have long accepted communist ideology; they are closely united under its banner.

In Korea national reunification precluding the Communists is inconceivable. To do so means negating stern reality and, in effect, is tantamount to perpetuating the division of the counttry.

We Communists always maintain that we will closely unite and cooperate with all the political parties, social organizations and individual personages that fight for peaceful reunification and national independence. We will cooperate with all persons, regardless of their past, if they come out for the peaceful reunification of the country.

Only the stooges of foreign imperialism who betray the interests of the nation will be afraid of Communists.

No political parties, social organization or individual personages can oppose "collaboration with the Communists" or reject free north-south elections if they are really concerned about the destiny of the nation and desire peaceful reunification.

There is no denying the fact that the most reasonable and realistic way to peaceful national reunification is to hold free north-south general elections on a democratic basis without any foreign interference. We appeal to all the political parties and social organizations and the people of all walks of life in south Korea to come out for holding such elections.

If the south Korean authorities still cannot agree to free north-south general elections for fear of the whole of south Korea being communized, then we must work out, to start with, even transitional measures for settling the burning problems of the nation.

As one of such measures, we propose that a Confederation of north and south Korea be instituted. We propose to establish the Confederation by way of setting up a supreme national committee composed of the representatives of the Government of the Democratic People's Republic of Korea and the Government of the "Republic of Korea" mainly to regulate the economic and cultural development of north and south Korea in a uniform manner, while retaining, for the time being, the present political systems in north and south Korea and maintaining the independent activities of the two governments.

The establishment of such a Confederation will enable the north and the south to understand and cooperate with each other by ensuring contacts and negotiations between them and removing mutual distrust. We consider that, if the free north-south general elections are held under such circumstances, the complete peaceful reunification of our country can be realized.

In particular, the establishment of such a Confederation will make it possible to save south Korea from economic ruin by having the supreme national committee consider economic and cultural matters beneficial to the whole nation and ensure economic and cultural exchanges and mutual cooperation between north and south Korea, even though the Confederation does not mean the formation of a united coalition government representing all social strata and therefore cannot exercise united state leadership.

It is the most urgent question at present to put the national economy in south Korea on the right track and improve the people's living which has been extremely deteriorated.

As we have consistently held and realities prove, this question cannot be solved unless the economic interchange between the north and the south is put into effect.

It is a rudiment of political economy that no country can develop light industry and agriculture or improve the people's living standards without heavy industry.

In our country such a heavy industry exists in the northern half. After liberation the working people in the north have, by their devoted labor, built powerful bases of heavy industry and laid the foundation of an independent national economy. We have also a large number of our own technical cadres and rich experience in economic construction.

We earnestly hope that the electricity, coal, steel, cement, timber, chemical fertilizer and various machines and equipment which are turned out in quantities in the north will be used for the rehabilitation of the economy and the improvement of the living conditions of the people in south Korea. We eagerly desire to share with our brothers and sisters in south Korea all the results and experience we have gained in developing the economy, science and technology.

Only by relying on the powerful economic foundation of the northern half can south Korea overcome the shortage of raw and other materials and funds, and develop its industry by putting the bankrupt industrial establishments into normal operation and building more factories. In the rural areas agricultural production can be quickly increased by carrying out large-scale irrigation projects and through an ample supply of fertilizer and farm machines. Without rehabilitating south Korea's industry and agriculture in this way it will be impossible to provide the millions of unemployed with jobs or to solve the pressing problem of the people's living.

It is only empty phrase-mongering to talk about saving south Korea from economic ruin without economic exchange and cooperation with the northern half.

Certain persons in south Korea blare that foreign capital should be introduced for the development of its economy and even advocate inviting Japanese capital which had long controlled the economy of our country. Through the bitter experience they had under Japanese imperialist rule, and through the realities of south Korea today, the Korean people know too well what the inroad of foreign capital means. Why must we invite foreign capital instead of turning to account the sufficient economic means that exist in our own country? Such insistence is tantamount only to attempting to push south Korea's economy further into an irreparable bankruptcy, an economy which has already been seriously devastated because of its subordination to U.S. monopoly capital.

If we exploit the rich resources of our country and develop our national economy in a uniform way, with the united strength of our 30 million people and on the basis of heavy industry in the north, we will all be able to live as well as others.

Anyone who is concerned about the wretched plight of the millions of unemployed and child beggars in south Korea and has the slightest concern about the future destinies of our ragged, hunger-stricken compatriots there, will not oppose the economic exchanges and economic cooperation between the north and the south.

If the south Korean authorities consider that even the Confederation we propose is still unacceptable to them, we once again propose that a purely economic commission composed of representatives of the business circles of north and south Korea be set up to exchange goods between the north and the south and to cooperate with and help each other in economic construction. Thus, we must, first of all, relieve the brothers and sisters in south Korea from hunger and poverty, setting aside the political question.

Along with the economic exchange between the north and the south, cultural interchange should be conducted on an extensive scale and the people allowed to travel freely.

The Korean nation is a homogenous nation with the same language, spoken and written, and has inherited the same historical and cultural traditions. However, we have been separated from each other for fifteen years, unable to visit each other, meet each other and even write to each other. Consequently, even our language is gradually changing in a different way in the two zones, and so are our culture and customs. Worse still, decadent Yankee culture and the American way of life hold sway and our national culture and the beautiful customs of our people are being trampled upon in south Korea.

This hinders the uniform development of our nation and, in particular, threatens the danger of plunging south Korea into an inescapable quagmire of corruption and degeneration.

We should under no circumstances allow ourselves to ruin the future destiny of the nation on account of political antagonism and thus commit crimes indelible for generations to come.

We once again propose that the mutual visit of cultural missions and mutual exchanges in science, culture, arts, sports and in all other fields be effected between the north and the south. At least, correspondence should be made possible between parents and children, brothers and sisters, relatives and friends, and the people allowed to travel freely across the country.

One of the important questions in improving the relations between the north and the south and particularly in normalizing the economic life in south Korea is the reduction of the armed forces. Today the maintenance of the huge army in south Korea is the greatest burden to the people.

We still hold that the U.S. army should be withdrawn from south Korea and the armies of north and south Korea be cut down to 100,000 or less respectively. This will constitute an important measure for easing tension in Korea and promoting peaceful reunification and, in particular, lighten the heavy burdens of military expenditure imposed upon the south Korean people. In our country an army 200,000 strong will be enough to discharge the duty of national defense.

All the above questions are burning issues awaiting urgent solution for the benefit of the Korean people and, above all, for delivering the south Korean people who are in dire straits. The current situation in south Korea does not brook even a moment's delay.

In order to solve these questions, representatives of north and south Korea should, first of all, get together and negotiate. Unscrupulously saying this is wrong, this is impossible, or something in a similar vein, even before meeting and talking with each other, is not a proper attitude favoring the solution of questions. Such an attitude benefits only the U.S. imperialists who are trying to keep our nation split and pit our people against each other and turn south Korea into their permanent colony. If we keep ourselves divided and our doors shut to each other, the situation will be further aggravated and south Korean people will suffer greater misery and hardships.

We propose to the south Korean authorities, political parties, social organizations and individual personages that representatives of north and south Korea meet at the earliest date in Pyongyang, Seoul or at Panmunjom to negotiate about all the above issues.

There is no reason why the Koreans, one and the same nation, should not meet together and negotiate. Why should we, people in the north, continue to hold talks with the Yankees about the question of our own country at Panmunjom, a place in our own land? Why should the south Korean people be deprived of their seats by the Yankees? The Yankees must pull out and Koreans should sit together and discuss the Korean question.

All political parties, social organizations and individual personages in south Korea should demand that the north and the south hold negotiations as soon as possible. All patriotic people in south Korea must struggle for economic and cultural exchange between the north and the south, for the reduction of the vast army of south Korea and for free north-south general elections.

The peaceful reunification of our country can by no means be easily achieved. We must not forget even for a moment that the U.S. imperialists, the ringleader of world reaction, are occupying south Korea. The peaceful reunification of the country can be achieved only by a persistent struggle of all the Korean people.

When the socialist forces are further strengthened in the northern half of the Republic and all the patriotic forces in south Korea firmly unite and turn out in the decisive struggle against the U.S. imperialists and their lackeys, we will be able to drive the U.S. imperialist aggressors out of south Korea and accomplish the great historic task of the peaceful reunification of our country.

Report on the Work of the Central Committee to the Fourth Congress of the Workers' Party of Korea
[Excerpt]

September 11, 1961

For the Peaceful Reunification of the Country

Comrades, during the period under review the situation in south Korea has changed tremendously. The great achievements in socialist construction in north Korea have decisively moved the balance of forces between revolution and counterrevolution in Korea in favor of the revolutionary forces.

The main trend in south Korean developments today is that while the revolutionary forces striving for the peaceful reunification of the country and for democracy grow continually stronger, the counterrevolutionary forces, isolated from the masses of the people, resort to the adventurist means of military terrorism in a last-ditch effort to find a way out of their blind alley.

In the spring of last year the south Korean people, no longer able to endure corruption and tyranny under U.S. imperialist colonial rule, finally rose up in a heroic resistance struggle for a new government and a new life, and they overthrew the Syngman Rhee regime. This was a great victory for the south

Koreans in their struggle to save the nation. It was a telling blow to the U.S. imperialist policy of aggression in Korea.

The April Popular Uprising marked a new turning point in the south Korean people's anti-U.S. struggle for national salvation. During this resistance the political consciousness of the south Korean people increased remarkably. With the momentum of their resistance, the spearhead of the struggle gradually began turning against U.S. imperialism.

The popular uprising and subsequent developments in south Korea show that the U.S. imperialists can never subdue the south Korean people, no matter how bloody the repression they resort to.

At the end of the Chang Myon regime the political and economic crises became extremely acute in south Korea. Life for the people became unbearable. Corruption and social disorder deteriorated conditions with each passing day.

The broad masses of the people came to realize all the more sharply that without the peaceful reunification of the country they could not free themselves from poverty, complete lack of rights, and colonial slavery. A mass struggle demanding north-south exchanges, the independent, peaceful reunification of the country, and north-south negotiation, developed with great force. South Korean youth and students came out with a proposal for north-south negotiations and exchanges, and the vast masses of the people rose in response. The general trend rapidly turned in favor of the masses of the people who supported the peaceful reunification of the country.

Driven into a tight corner, the U.S. imerialists and the south Korean reactionaries embarked upon the adventurist path of setting up a fascist military dictatorship to try to maintain their precarious rule.

The establishment of the dictatorial military regime in south Korea testifies to the fact that the U.S. imperialists' position in Korea is weakened, not strengthened. This is nothing more than the death-bed frenzy of the doomed. No matter what they do, the U.S. imperialists can never save the irretrievable, disintegrating colonial system in south Korea. The fascist military rule rather inflames the struggle of the people and will hasten the ultimate collapse of U.S. imperialist colonial rule over south Korea.

South Korea today has turned into a land of darkness where all democratic freedoms and rights have been denied—into a slaughter house of the people rampant with mass terrorism and murder. The south Korean military regime has disbanded all political parties and social organizations, closed down all the progressive organs of the press, and has already arrested, imprisoned, or massacred more than 100,000 patriots and innocent people.

Political chaos and unrest are steadily growing in south Korea and the contradictions and conflicts within the military circles are sharpening to an astonishing degree. The south Korean economy is going from bad to worse, and mass starvation is sweeping the whole of the south. It can never be otherwise as long as U.S. imperialism dominates south Korea.

The military rulers of south Korea are now clamoring about "reform," "building a self-reliant economy," and "relief for the people." But these are nothing but deceptions designed to placate the people's discontent and intensify fascist suppression. Developments in south Korea are vividly revealing that such slogans are nothing but empty promises.

In south Korea power is completely held by the U.S. imperialists. Until the colonial rule of U.S. imperialism is abolished, the south Korean regime, no matter who may seize power, will inevitably represent the interests of the U.S. imperialists and their collaborators—the landlords and the comprador capitalists—and the position of the south Korean people cannot be expected to improve.

By means of "aid," the U.S. imperialists have seized the main arteries of south Korea's economy, subordinated them to their military purposes and completely blocked the road to independent development of the national economy in south Korea. Reduced to a military appendage of U.S. imperialism, the south Korean economy is faced with unavoidable ruin.

South Korea's industry is bankrupt. Oppressed by American monopoly capital and comprador capital, national industry is disintegrating even more and is steadily advancing toward bankruptcy and ruin. The overwhelming majority of the national capitalists' enterprises consist of medium- and small-sized units and at present, more than 80 percent of these are either not functioning or are operating below capacity.

Today, south Korea's meager light industry is almost entirely dependent on American machinery, equipment and raw material.

The bulk consists of war industry which provides supplementary war materials on the spot to the American mercenaries. The masters of this war industry are the comprador capitalists under U.S. protection.

South Korean markets are overflowing with U.S. commodities from overseas, and imports from U.S. "aid" account for 80 percent of south Korea's total volume of imports, which is 20 times the total volume of exports.

Thus, south Korea today remains a backward agrarian region without an independent industry.

Alongside the bankruptcy of industry, the south Korean rural economy has also been utterly devastated.

Feudal landlordism still prevails in the countryside. The bulk of the "distributed land" for the peasants has again been massed in the hands of landlords and rich farmers, and the peasants are subjected to ruthless feudal exploitation.

The pillage and exploitation by the U.S. imperialists and the landlords have not only held back the development of south Korea's agriculture but have sapped it to the limit. Compared with pre-liberation years, cultivated land has gone down 200,000 *chongbo* and the area sown, 400,000 *chongbo*. U.S. imperialist aggressive troops have requisitioned more than 100,000 *chongbo* of land from the south Korean peasants for military use. With industry bankrupt and the rural economy completely disintegrated, agricultural technology is horribly backward.

The destruction and stagnation of agricultural productive forces have caused a sharp decline in production. Grain output in 1960 dropped to two-thirds of the 1937 pre-liberation level.

Economic bankruptcy and cruel exploitation by the landlords and comprador capitalists have reduced the working people to a state of indescribable misery.

More than 6 million working people, that is, half of the labor force of south Korea, are chronically unemployed or semi-unemployed.

The regime in south Korea annually appropriates more than 70 percent of its budget for military expenditure. To cover this, it is raising taxes even more. Soaring inflation caused by oversized military expenditure weighs heavily on the working people. As of July 1961, the volume of currency in circulation had increased 206 times and commodity prices 126 times in comparison with 1949. The tax burden of the south Korean people rose more than 10 times in the seven years after the war. The workers are forced to work 10-18 hours a day, while their wages are less than one-third of what they need to meet minimum costs of living.

The broad masses of peasants have been reduced to debt slaves of landlords and usurers. The amount of peasants' debts soared 20-fold in the postwar period. Each year tens of thousands of peasant families are ruined and are forced to desist from farming. Since industry cannot absorb the ruined rural population, most of them are wandering beggars.

Such is the outcome of 16 years' rule by the U.S. imperialists and their stooges. Such is the result of U.S. "aid" to south Korea.

The U.S. army's occupation of south Korea and their policy of aggression are the main obstacles to the peaceful reunification of our country and the democratic development of south Korean society. They are the root of all the present misfortunes and sufferings of the south Korean people. The U.S. imperialists have converted south Korea into their colony and military base; they are constantly menacing peace in Korea and are doing all they can to obstruct our country's peaceful reunification. They have utterly ruined the south Korean economy, plunged the people of the south into the depths of famine and poverty, and turned the whole of south Korea into a living hell of terrorism and tyranny. Countless patriotic people and innocent countrymen are shedding their blood because of the atrocities of the U.S. robbers, and our sisters are insulted and walked over in south Korea.

Today the U.S. imperialists are stepping up their war preparations under the pretext of "protecting" south Korea from "communist aggression," and they are viciously scheming to drive the south Korean people into a fratricidal conflict.

U.S. imperialism is the principal target of the struggle of the people in south Korea and the sworn enemy of all the Korean people. As long as U.S. armed forces occupy the south, we cannot expect a durable peace in Korea and the peaceful reunification of the country, and the south Korean people cannot win genuine freedom and liberation.

In maintaining their colonial rule in south Korea, the U.S. imperialists rely on the landlords, comprador capitalists and reactionary bureaucrats who serve them as guides and faithful allies in their aggression. The landlord class, under U.S. imperialist protection, ruthlessly exploits and suppresses the peasant masses. The comprador capitalists make fortunes by bringing in American commodities and capital, by plundering our country's natural resources and selling them to their masters, and by supplying the American mercenary troops with war materials.

Thus, the revolution in south Korea is a national-liberation revolution against imperialism, and is, at the same time, a democratic revolution against the feudal forces. The basic demand of this revolution is to drive the aggressive forces of U.S. imperialism out of Korea, shatter its colonial rule, and achieve both democratic development in south Korean society and the reunification of the country.

Comrades, to carry on the anti-imperialist, anti-feudal struggle successfully and to emerge victorious, the south Korean people must have a revolutionary party which takes Marxism-Leninism as its guideline and represents the interests of the workers, peasants and other broad sections of the popular masses. Without such a political party, it is impossible to set forth a clear-cut fighting program for the people, to solidly unite the revolutionary masses, and to carry on the popular struggle in an organized way.

Since there was no revolutionary party and no clear-cut program of struggle and since, as a result, the workers and peasants, the main masses, failed to take part extensively in the resistance, the April Popular Uprising could not be carried through in an organized way; and the south Korean people were inevitably robbed by new puppets of U.S. imperialism of the gains they had paid for with their blood. In addition, leadership by a revolutionary party was lacking, and the masses of workers, peasants and soldiers were not awakened. Therefore, the south Korean people failed to prevent the seizure of power by fascist elements in the upper strata of the army and to organize an effective counterattack against the enemy's onslaught on democratic rights.

The people in south Korea must learn from this bitter experience. They must have an independent workers' and peasants' party—a party deeply rooted in the broad masses—and they must win legal status for it.

This political party, to be organized by the working people in south Korea, will have to unite all patriotic forces and fight for the realization of a thoroughly anti-imperialist, anti-feudal program, and for the satisfaction of the urgent demands of the south Korean people.

The primary task before the south Korean people is to fight against the occupation of south Korea by the U.S. imperialists and to struggle for the withdrawal of the U.S. forces of aggression.

The south Korean people must thoroughly expose and smash the sinister design of the U.S. imperialists to pit our brothers against each other under the pretext of checking "communist aggression." The Korean people want no fratricidal conflict. There may be different ideas and different political points of view among us, but the differences should not be an obstacle to the country's peaceful reunification, much less a cause of war. The phrase "communist aggression" is a lie invented by the U.S. imperialists and is nothing but a smoke screen to justify their occupation of south Korea, cover up their intention to invade all Korea, and to hoodwink the people in the south. The south Korean people must rise up in an all-people resistance to frustrate U.S. imperialist policies of aggression and war preparations. Young people must fight against forced conscription. Workers must organize slowdowns and strikes to obstruct the enemy production of armaments and transport of war supplies. And the entire people in south Korea must fight against the construction of military bases and installations.

The south Korean people must resolutely condemn and curb the bandit actions of the U.S. troops—the contempt, plunder and slaughter of our fellow countrymen—and bridle the aggressors so that they cannot operate arbitrarily. They must unconditionally refuse to collaborate in any way with the U.S. army of aggression and should not give them even a single grain of rice or a single drop of water. The aggressors must be made to tremble before the resistance of the enraged people, and not a single foot of our land should be left for these aggressors to stand on. Thus, the U.S. troops of aggression should be forced to withdraw as soon as possible, all the shackling military and economic pacts concluded between south Korea and the United States repudiated, and the U.S. colonial fetters shaken off once and for all.

When all the patriotic forces in south Korea are firmly united as one and rise up resolutely in the anti-U.S. struggle, the U.S. imperialists will find it impossible to hang on in our territory. And they will be driven out of south Korea without fail.

At the same time the south Korean people must struggle against exploitation and oppression by the landlords and comprador capitalists who are in league with U.S. imperialists. They must also fight for the democratic development of south Korean society.

At present there is an urgent demand in south Korea to democratize social and political life, carry out democratic reforms in economic and cultural areas, and resolve the problem of the people's living conditions.

The south Korean military regime has completely deprived the people of even the most elementary democratic rights, binding them hand and foot.

South Korean military rulers are intensifying their fascist suppression of the people, arresting and jailing large numbers of patriots at random on the pretext of combating communism. They have gone so far as to perpetrate the intolerable outrage of sentencing reporters to death merely because they stood for withdrawal of the U.S. imperialists and for reunification with-out outside interference.

The people in south Korea must smash the fascist dictatorship and fight for their democratic freedom and rights. Freedom of speech, press, association, assembly, demonstrations and strikes must be guaranteed and freedom of activities for all political parties and social organizations must be restored. The barbarous terrorism of the military regime must be stopped immediately. All patriotic political prisoners and innocent people under arrest or in prison must be released immediately, and both agents of U.S. imperialism and traitors to the nation must be punished.

Solution of the land problem is one of the most important tasks confronting the democratic revolution in south Korea. Unless this problem is settled and agricultural productive forces are freed from their feudal fetters, the peasant masses, who make up more than 70 percent of the population in south Korea, can neither be saved from hunger and poverty, nor stabilize their living conditions.

The south Korean peasantry must unite in one body and struggle to enforce a democratic agrarian reform and to put an end to the system of feudal exploitation. Land should and must be owned by the peasants who till it. The landlords' land must be confiscated and distributed without payment among the landless and land-poor peasants so that they can realize their age-old desire for land. Those who have opposed U.S. imperialism and contributed to the cause of the country's peaceful reunification may be compensated for their land.

Land requisitioned by the U.S. occupation forces for military use must be immediately restored to the peasants.

A thoroughgoing democratic agrarian reform must be enforced; at the same time land must be extensively reclaimed and divided for free among land-poor peasants and unemployed people who had been forced to abandon farming.

Exploitation of the peasants through various kinds of usury must be prohibited; their land debts, as well as all the debts of the poor peasants, must also be cancelled.

The liquidation of feudal relations in the south Korean countryside will not only pave the way for the development of the agricultural productive forces and ensure the improvement of the peasants' living conditions but will also create favorable conditions for the development of national industry.

Without an independent national industry neither the people's well-being can be prompted nor national independence achieved. The factories, mines, railway facilities and banks owned by U.S. imperialists, comprador capitalists and traitors to the nation should be confiscated and nationalized to smash the economic bases of foreign imperialism and the traitorous domestic forces and to develop national industry. In particular, middle and small entrepreneurs must be allowed to develop freely by protecting their sector of the economy and ensuring them raw materials, funds and markets.

The south Korean workers must struggle for the enforcement of an eight-hour day, social security, a wage increase and the improvement of working conditions. Jobs must be given to the millions of unemployed as soon as possible and the workers' wages raised to meet, at the very least, the minimum cost of living. Commodity prices must also be stabilized, and the tax burden of the working people drastically alleviated together with the abolition of miscellaneous charges.

There is no work even for the small number of scientists and technicians in south Korea, much less conditions and freedom for their scientific research. The minds of the people are poisoned by reactionary, decadent American culture, while the culture peculiar to our nation is trampled upon and left to rot. Scientists and people working in culture and art must fight the penetration of reactionary American culture, struggle to improve their living conditions, and bravely strive to build a democratic national culture which serves the nation's independent development and the people's interests.

South Korean student youth and intellectuals should fight against the militarization and commercialization of schools and for a democratic reform of the educational system. Universal, compulsory primary education must be enforced to educate all children of school age at state expense, and an extensive adult education system should be introduced to give the working people an opportunity to learn and to eliminate illiteracy.

In south Korea today various epidemics and chronic diseases are rampant owing to the people's wretched living conditions and the rulers' criminal indifference to public health. Countless numbers of sick people, denied medical treatment, are suffering and dying. A system of free medical service must be instituted to protect the health of the people, and state measures must be taken to eliminate different kinds of epidemics.

To democratize all aspects of life for people in south Korea, one of the major tasks is to ensure to the women of the south social status and rights equal to those of men. Women should be liberated from the humiliation of being mistreated and despised, their personal dignity should be respected, and they should be guaranteed an equal opportunity for education. They should be actively incorporated into the work of society, and they should be included under the principle, equal pay for equal work.

The U.S. imperialists are keeping 700,000 mercenary soldiers in south Korea. Command of the "ROK army" is in the hands of the U.S. imperialists: its commanders are American generals. The overwhelming majority of the south Korean army are peasants and workers in uniform. They are young working people pressganged into the "ROK army" by the minions of U.S. imperialism.

Men in the south Korean army are forced to level their guns at their fellow countrymen in north Korea and to fire upon their parents and brothers who fight for freedom and survival.

In north Korea there is no enemy of the "ROK army." The People's Army, an army of workers and peasants, never wants to fight its brothers in south Korea. The real enemies of the "ROK army" are the U.S. imperialists, who occupy our territory, and their flunkies.

The south Korean army should no longer remain a blind tool of the U.S. imperialists in their suppression of the people's patriotic and democratic movements and their invasion of the whole of Korea. Rather, it should become a national army, a people's army, defending the interests of the workers, peasants and the rest of the broad popular masses against the foreign imperialists. Command of the "ROK army" should be wrested from the hands of the U.S. imperialists. The anti-popular military service system should be abolished. And the fascist military system should be turned into a democratic one.

The rank and file and the junior officers of the "ROK army" must not be deceived by the pernicious plot of the U.S. imperialists to make Koreans fight Koreans. They must come over to the side of the people, resolutely reject the orders of the American commanders and the traitorous clique in the upper crust of the "ROK army," and fight against the U.S. imperialists and their minions.

People can win freedom and liberation only through their own struggle. The south Korean people have a glorious tradition of heroic struggle against foreign imperialist aggressive forces and against domestic exploiters. The liberation struggles of the popular masses, such as the Kabo Peasant War, the March First Movement, the June 10th Independence Movement and the Kwangju Student Incident, have been waged without stop, and telling blows have been struck at the oppressors. When the vast majority of the popular masses rise up in a body to struggle against their oppressors, any imperialist stronghold can be smashed. The U.S. imperialists bragged that the Syngman Rhee regime was the strongest anti-communist regime in Asia. But it was overthrown precisely by the mass struggle of the south Korean people.

Workers, peasants, youth and students, intellectuals and the broad masses of the people in south Korea must valiantly rise up in the struggle against U.S. imperialism and its stooges for democracy and for the right to exist.

Comrades, the only way for the south Korean people to completely free themselves from their present tragic situation is to drive out the U.S. army, overthrow the fascist dictatorship and reunify the country peacefully. During their history of tribulations since the liberation sixteen years ago, the south Korean people have come to realize keenly that they cannot go on living with the country divided into north and south.

The only way to rehabilitate and develop the economy and

improve the people's living conditions in south Korea is to achieve the country's reunification by the united strength of north and south Korea.

Peaceful reunification of our country is the unanimous desire of all Koreans and the supreme national task which must be solved without delay.

The position of our Party on the question of Korean reunification is clear. The Party has consistently maintained that the question of reunifying our country should be solved independently by peaceful means based on democratic principles. The Korean people can and must themselves achieve peaceful national reunification.

To fully solve the question of our country's reunification, a unified government should be established by free elections on democratic principles throughout the whole of Korea without any interference from the outside forces. Separate elections in south Korea alone can never alter the situation. A unified government truly representing the people's will can be formed only through all-Korea elections in which the people in the northern half, and the workers, peasants and various other strata of the people in south Korea participate; and only by forming such a government can the south Korean people gain their freedom and rights and change the conditions in which they live.

We consider that such elections should be held on the principle of universal, equal and direct suffrage by secret ballot.

The reunification of Korea is an internal affair of our nation which must be decided by the Korean people of their own free will. There can be no expression of the people's free will as long as the country is occupied by the imperialist aggressive forces and outside interference is tolerated. The prerequisite for genuine free elections is to force the U.S. imperialist army of aggression out of Korea and to reject any interference from outside.

At the same time, freedom of political activities should be guaranteed throughout north and south Korea. All political parties, social organizations and individual public figures in both parts should be able to openly announce their political platforms, express their political views before the people without any restriction, and engage in free activity wherever they are in the country. Only when these conditions are ensured can the Korean people establish a unified government through genuine free elections.

The proposals of our Party and the Government of the Republic on the peaceful reunification of the country are most reasonable, realistic and fair. Our reunification program enjoys the ardent support of the entire Korean people and the approval of the peace-loving peoples of all countries of the world. Only the U.S. imperialists and their followers, the traitorous reactionary forces, prevent the holding of free, general elections throughout north and south Korea and stand opposed to the peaceful reunification of the country.

Frustrating the obstructive maneuvers of the enemy, all patriotic peoples in south Korea should courageously struggle for general elections throughout north and south Korea. Workers, peasants and other sectors of the people in the south should wage a stubborn fight for the withdrawal of the U.S. army of aggression and for the attainment of the independent, democratic and peaceful reunification of the country.

Although the Korean people's struggle for the peaceful reunification of the country is complicated by difficult twists and turns, the revolutionary situation is developing in our favor. All Koreans are eagerly awaiting the great event of national reunification, and the day of its realization is drawing nearer.

To fulfill this national aspiration the Korean people in the north and south should unite all their forces and enter the struggle against the U.S. imperialists' occupation of south Korea and for the country's peaceful reunification.

The most crucial necessity in the development of the revolution today is to form an anti-U.S., national-salvation united front in south Korea, embracing all patriotic forces. The workers, peasants, urban petty bourgeoisie, youth and students, intellectuals and even the national capitalists in south Korea are all suffering from the partition of the country and U.S. imperialist colonial rule. They are all linked by common national interests. The forces of all these classes and strata should be solidly united and directed in struggle against U.S. imperialism, the principal enemy of the Korean people. Only by doing so, can the south Korean people repel the common enemy, win the struggle for liberation and realize the cause of national reunification.

It is of utmost importance in forming an anti-U.S. national salvation united front to strengthen the worker-peasant alliance under the leadership of the working class. The worker-peasant alliance should become the political and social basis of the united front.

While consolidating the worker-peasant alliance, efforts should be made to strengthen solidarity with the youth and students and intellectuals. They should be more extensively drawn into the anti-U.S., national-salvation struggle and should be made to go deeply among the broad masses of the people, including workers and peasants, and keep close ties with the popular masses.

Thus, the U.S. imperialists and their lackeys should be thoroughly isolated, all the patriotic, democratic strata in south Korea should be rallied under the banner of independent, peaceful reunification, and unity should be achieved between the patriotic, democratic forces of south Korea and the patriotic, socialist forces of north Korea.

We shall march hand in hand with those who struggle against U.S. imperialism without asking about their past, their class background, social status, political views and religious beliefs. We will warmly welcome even those who in the past committed crimes against the homeland and the people provided they repent their crimes and openly support the country's peaceful reunification. And we will not fail to embrace them at all times after the reunification.

We are now living in the age of the disintegration of the imperialist colonial system, in the great era of national-liberation revolution. Hundreds of millions of people who only yesterday were oppressed and exploited by foreign aggressors have won their freedom and independence, throwing off the colonial yoke. All the peoples of the world who groan under imperialist oppression are launching valiant struggles against the aggressors. The liquidation of colonialism is a trend of the times which no force can hold back.

How can our nation, with its long history and time-honored culture, put up with U.S. imperialist colonial rule and tolerate national humiliation and persecution in this great age of national-liberation revolution?

All those who love their country and people should unite and rise up in the save-the-nation struggle to expel the aggressors and reunify the country peacefully.

Once the entire Korean people firmly unite to combat the U.S. imperialist aggressors and their lackeys, they will be able to defeat the enemy, no matter how desperate he may be, winning a glorious victory.

The U.S. imperialists will be driven out of Korea and the cause of national reunification will unquestionably be achieved by the united might of the whole nation.

On the Immediate Tasks of the Government of the Democratic People's Republic of Korea
[Excerpt]

Speech Delivered at the First Session of the Third Supreme People's Assembly, October 23, 1962

Comrade Deputies, the great successes achieved in the construction of socialism in the northern half of the Republic are exerting a great revolutionary influence on the people in south Korea who are under the colonial rule of U.S. imperialism. These successes are moving the balance of forces between revolution and counterrevolution in Korea more and more in favor of the former.

Inspired by the great victories achieved by their north Korean brothers in socialist construction, the south Korean people rose up in a heroic struggle and overthrew the Syngman Rhee regime that had ridden roughshod over them for 12 years, and now they maintain a determined struggle against U.S. imperialist colonial rule and the military dictatorship.

Developments in south Korea since the April Popular Uprising show that no "legal" replacement of the regime nor establishment of a terrorist dictatorship by sheer force enables the U.S. imperialists to tide over the political and economic crises in south Korea or suppress the people's struggle there for democratic freedom, the right to live and the peaceful reunification of the country.

Despite bloody repression by the U.S. imperialists and the south Korean military regime, anti-U.S. sentiments are mounting among the broad masses of the people in south Korea, and the patriotic and democratic forces are gradually growing stronger.

In the year and a half following the seizure of power by the military fascist clique, the political and economic crises in south Korea have deepened. The economy has declined further, the people's living standards are deteriorating, and corruption and social disorder is increasing.

In south Korea all the political parties and social organizations have been dissolved, and martial law has been in force for more than a year now.

While launching an unprecedented barbarous attack on the democratic freedom of the people, the south Korean military regime is trying hard to quell the people's discontent, making a lot of talk about the "construction of a self-reliant economy," a "five-year plan for economic development," or "relief for the impoverished." But no one expects that the south Korean military regime, a mere tool of U.S. imperialist colonial rule, will ever do any of these things. It has already become quite evident that all this is nothing but absolute nonsense.

The economy of south Korea under U.S. imperialist occupation is in a state of irretrievable ruin.

Having seized the key branches of the economy of south Korea, the U.S. imperialists have reduced it to their military appendage and have totally destroyed the south Korean national economy.

Under the pressure of U.S. monopoly capital and comprador capital, national industry in south Korea has been completely stifled and ruined. Owing to the increasing shortage of raw materials and funds and to the growing market difficulties, within just one year after the setting up of the military regime, industrial production fell by 9 percent.

South Korean agriculture has also been totally devastated. The vast peasant masses are still being harshly exploited under the feudalistic landlord system. Plunder and exploitation by the U.S. imperialists and the landlords have ruined south Korean agricultrue severely. Both the total arable land and the area actually planted are steadily decreasing, and agricultural production is still based on backward, medieval techniques. Thus, south Korea, formerly a granary, has been converted into a region of chronic famine and has to import 4 to 5 million *sok* of U.S. surplus grain every year.

The south Korean people are living in untold misery due to economic bankruptcy on all fronts and cruel exploitation at the hands of the U.S. imperialists, the landlords, and the comprador capitalists.

Millions of working people have lost their jobs and are wandering in the streets. As no measures have been taken for their relief, they hover on the verge of starvation. Sixty percent of all the able-bodied men in south Korea today are either unemployed or underemployed.

The people have been totally impoverished. Nevertheless, south Korea's rulers are exacting increasing taxes from the working people to cover their huge military expenditures. The tax burden on the south Korean people in 1962 increased 43 percent since 1960. As a result of the acute inflation caused by snowballing military spending, commodity prices are steadily rising. As of July this year, commodity prices in south Korea were up by more than 20 percent as against the end of 1960.

The U.S. imperialists have thoroughly disorganized the south Korean economy and brought unspeakable suffering to the south Korean people, transforming the whole of south Korea into a living hell where mass terror and tyranny prevail. The people's lives and property are constantly threatened by the American robbers, and our compatriots, our brothers and sisters are insulted and murdered by the aggressors. Mass starvation is sweeping south Korea, and almost every day many people starve to death.

This is the consequence of the colonial rule of U.S. imperialism in south Korea and of the traitorous policy of the south Korean rulers.

The only way to save the present situation in south Korea and to relieve the people there from hunger and poverty is to drive out the U.S. troops and achieve national reunification.

Unless the complete independence and reunification of the country is achieved, the Korean people will not be able to live in peace for one minute, nor will the people in south Korea be able to free themselves from their present misery. The achievement of the great work of national reunification is the unanimous desire of all Koreans, in north and south. It is the supreme national task.

Reunification of our country should be achieved independently and by peaceful means without the interference of any outside forces after driving out foreign troops.

Having turned south Korea into their colony and military base and driven south Korean society into the depths of ruin, the U.S. imperialists are constantly threatening peace in Korea by aggravating tension. They are obstructing the reunification of our country by resorting to all sorts of sinister schemes.

The occupation of south Korea by the U.S. imperialists and their aggressive policy are the root causes of all the misfortunes and sufferings of the people in south Korea; they are the main obstacle to the progress of south Korean society and the peaceful reunification of our country.

History has never seen the achievement of independence and reunification when a country is occupied by foreign aggressor troops and is suffering outside interference.

Only by driving the U.S. army of aggression out of south Korea will it be possible to deliver the south Koreans from hunger, poverty, and colonial slavery, and to realize the national desire to reunify our divided country. Those who talk about the reunification of the country while justifying the occupation of south Korea by U.S. troops are, in fact, the opponents of reunification and agents of imperialism.

There is no reason whatsoever for the U.S. imperialists to station their troops in south Korea, nor can it be justified in any way. The U.S. army must pull out of south Korea and the Korean question must be settled by the Korean people themselves.

The U.S. imperialists are clamoring that the U.S. army must be stationed in south Korea in order to check "communist aggression from the north." But they can deceive no one with such a lie.

Our Party and the Government of the Republic are consistent in their efforts for the peaceful settlement of the Korean question. We have no intention of marching south, we have no intention of solving the question of Korean reunification by force of arms.

"Communist aggression from the north" is nothing but a subterfuge of the U.S. imperialists to cover up their sinister design to continue the occupation of south Korea, extend their invasion to the whole of Korea and further their aggression in Asia. The people in south Korea should thoroughly expose and frustrate the vicious scheming of the U.S. imperialists to invade all of Korea by pitting Koreans against Koreans.

We consider that the United Nations has no right to discuss the Korean question nor has it any right to meddle in the domestic affairs of our country. The Korean question should not be discussed by foreigners in New York or Washington; it should be discussed in Pyongyang or Seoul by the Koreans themselves.

The question of Korean reunification is an internal affair of the Korean people, and it can be settled by them alone. What grounds do foreign countries have for interfering in the domestic affairs of Korea, and how can they possibly settle the internal affairs of our nation? To try to achieve the reunification of the country by relying on outside forces is an illusion and is tantamount to leaving the whole of Korea open to imperialist aggression.

The Korean people can, and must reunify their country through their own efforts.

Reunification of our country is a complicated and difficult task that cannot be performed easily. Only through a hard and long-drawn-out struggle can we accomplish the great task of national reunification, for the U.S. imperialists, the overlords of world imperialism, have occupied south Korea and are now plotting frantically to unleash a new war, pursuing a policy of aggression against the whole of Korea and Asia.

We should carry out the independent, peaceful reunification of our country in a gradual way, through a series of intermediary steps, on the condition that foreign troops are with-drawn from south Korea.

In order to achieve the country's reunification, it is of paramount importance to eliminate the tension between north and south created by the U.S. imperialists.

The U.S. army should be withdrawn, a peace agreement should be concluded between the north and south on refraining from attack on each other and the armed forces of each be re-duced to 100,000 or less. We have proposed this on a number of occasions and have done everything in our power to achieve this end.

Neither north or south should increase their armed forces nor their armaments; instead, the armed forces should be re-duced and tension eliminated so that both sides can work to build up the national economy and improve the standards of the people.

The U.S. imperialists maintain a 700,000-strong mercenary army in south Korea, grinding the people down. This huge military force in the south has nothing to do with national de-fense; it is merely an instrument of U.S. imperialism for carrying out a policy of aggression. It imposes an unbearably heavy bur-den on the people in south Korea and seriously threatens peace in Korea.

The conclusion of a peace agreement between north and south Korea and the reduction of their respective armed forces would, above all, mean relief for the people in the south from the heavy burdens of military expenditure and removal of the tension that has been artificially created between north and south, thereby creating an atmosphere of mutual trust.

The withdrawal of all foreign troops from south Korea, the conclusion of a peace agreement between north and south, and the reduction of their armed forces would prove to be important initial steps toward the reunification of the country.

Elimination of tension between the north and south would enable us to take a further step and enter into economic and cultural exchange and cooperation.

A burning issue in south Korea today is the rehabilitation of its devastated economy and the improvement of the miserable living conditions of the people there. The only way of solving this problem is to establish economic and cultural relations and promote exchange and cooperation between the north and south.

Under the leadership of our Party, the people in the northern half have, through a heroic struggle, laid the foundations of industrialization and built a solid basis for an independent national economy. The economic foundations we have already established in the northern half of the Republic are a sure guarantee for the independent development of the national economy of Korea as a whole.

Only when economic cooperation and exchange between north and south Korea make it possible to take advantage of the economic foundations built in north Korea, can the industry and agriculture of south Korea be rehabilitated and developed, can the millions of unemployed be given jobs, and the life of its people generally improved.

We think it is necessary to organize an economic committee composed of representatives of north and south Korea for the purpose of effectively carrying out north-south exchanges.

The south Korean authorities, contrary to the will of the Korean people, are now trying to find a way out by bringing in foreign capital. The introduction of foreign capital leads to a state of dependence and national bankruptcy. This will only result in plunging the already ruined south Korean economy deeper into the abyss of hopeless destruction and in making south Korea more and more dependent on imperialism. The outcome of U.S. "aid" to south Korea over the 17 years since liberation is a striking proof of this.

When the north and the south combine their efforts to exploit our rich domestic resources, relying on the powerful economic foundations of north Korea, our nation will not only be able to stand on its own feet, but also build a modern, rich, powerful and independent state.

When exchange and mutual cooperation between the north and the south are put into effect, we shall be able to take another step toward epoch-making measures for the initial reunification of the country.

In order to achieve initial reunification, we consider the establishment of the Confederation already proposed by our Party and the Government of the Republic to be a reasonable step.

Our proposal of a Confederation is aimed at setting up a Supreme National Committee, composed of representatives of the Government of the Democratic Peoples Republic of Korea and the Government of the "Republic of Korea" to jointly solve matters of concern to the whole nation, while leaving intact the present socio-political systems in north and south Korea and ensuring the independence of action of the two governments.

Under the Confederation, neither north nor south shall interfere in the internal affairs of the other, nor shall one impose its will upon the other. North and south Korea shall act freely according to their respective political beliefs and jointly settle only those problems of common national interest on which agreement has been reached through the confederative body.

Unlike a confederation of nations with different languages, customs and cultures, the Confederation we propose would be a coming together of two temporarily divided parts of a single nation which has had the same language, customs and culture throughout its long history. Therefore, the establishment of the Confederation of north and south will make it possible for us to do tremendous work for the prosperity of the country and the benefit of the nation—developing the national economy and culture in a coordinated way and jointly exploiting all domestic resources, appearing as one nation in various fields of international activity, and so forth.

The establishment of the Confederation will also promote contacts and mutual understanding, strengthen politico-economic ties between north and south and create an atmosphere of national amity, thereby initiating a very favorable phase in the achievement of the complete peaceful reunification of our country.

We can, and must, achieve the complete reunification of our country by taking these intermediary steps.

As our Party and Government have made clear time and again, in order to achieve that goal, a unified central government, representing all strata of people in north and south Korea, must be set up on the basis of free elections throughout the whole country, conducted on democratic principles.

The guarantee of freedom to travel and freedom of political activity for the people both in north and south Korea, as well as the rejection of any interference by external forces, are prerequisites for free all-Korea elections.

In south Korea the suppression of the patriotic and democratic movement of the people must be brought to an end at once, and freedom of speech, the press, association and assembly, and freedom to demonstrate and to strike must be ensured. All political parties and social organizations outlawed by the military regime must be restored and complete freedom of their activities ensured.

All political parties, social organizations and individual public figures in north and south Korea must be guaranteed freedom of activity in all parts of the country and the freedom to express their political views before the people without any restriction whatsoever.

Only when these conditions are ensured can the Korean people establish an all-Korea central government through genuinely free elections and achieve the complete peaceful reunification of the country.

This stand of the Workers' Party of Korea and the Government of the Democratic People's Republic of Korea on the reunification of the country reflects the interests of the whole nation and the will of the entire Korean people.

Certain persons in south Korea are dead set against independent, peaceful reunification of our country, alleging that its realization would lead to the "communization" of south Korea. Whether the ideal of communism is realized in south Korea or not is a matter to be decided by the south Korean people themselves, and no one can impose it on them. No progressive ideas and social systems can be imposed from outside; they are chosen by people themselves of their own free will. To oppose the reunification of the country on the pretext of fearing the "communization" of south Korea is to go against the entire people's earnest desire for reunification and to betray the vital interests of the whole nation.

The rulers in south Korea still persist in their old "theory of wiping out communism for reunification" and are prattling on about building up their strength to "prevail over communism."

Attempts have already been made to wipe out communism and impose the colonial system on the whole of Korea through the power of imperialism, but this goal has proved absolutely unattainable. For almost 40 years, Japanese imperialist colonial rule could not stamp out the communist movement in Korea. Syngman Rhee who had made the extermination of communism his lifetime task could not achieve his goal even though banking on the power of U.S. imperialism. Rather he was forsaken by the people and met his downfall for his crimes. Some of those die-hards in south Korea who are bent on anti-communism must learn these lessons of history. Anyone daring to follow in the wake of Syngman Rhee will surely meet the same fate as his predecessor.

The reunification of our country is not a question of conquerors and conquered, but of the restoration of national unity in an originally united nation by completely freeing itself from the yoke of imperialism.

The pipe dream of "wiping out communism" or "prevailing over communism" is not only past all hope of realization. It is also a very harmful idea aimed at preventing the reunification of the country and perpetuating a divided nation.

The stand of our Party and the Government of the Republic on the reunification of the country is irrefutable; it is the most fair and reasonable one.

Anyone who truly defends the interests of the nation and is concerned about the future of the country should fight for an improved life for the people in south Korea, today in dire straits, and for the country's peaceful reunification. This is the solemn national duty of every Korean.

In order to achieve reunification of the country it is most important to promote mutual understanding, and achieve national amity and solidarity between north and south in every way. Antagonism and enmity between the north and south and the failure to achieve national unity only benefit the U.S. imperialists. The imperialist aggressors fear our national awakening and unity more than anything else. They resort to every vile scheme to undermine national unity, sow discord and create antagonism within the nation, with the object of achieving their goal of aggression.

All the patriotic people of north and south Korea should decisively smash the U.S. imperialist policy of dividing the nation and close ranks under the banner of national reunification.

We will unite and work together with anyone, regardless of his past record and political beliefs, as long as he defends the interests of the nation and works for the reunification of the homeland.

We can join hands even with those now in power in south Korea if they stop betraying the nation by conspiring with the foreign aggressors, stop repressing the people, and join in the struggle for independent, peaceful reunification of the country. But if they refuse to do so and continue to fawn upon the foreign forces and tag along behind them, repressing the people's just struggle for democracy and the right to live, and if they keep on obstructing the country's reunification to the last, it will be an indelible crime never to be erased from our nation's memory, and they will not be able to escape the stern judgement of the entire Korean people.

Unity should be achieved between the socialist forces of the northern half of the Republic and the patriotic, democratic forces of south Korea, and the whole nation should unite firmly in the fight against U.S. imperialist aggression and for the peaceful reunification of our country.

All sectors of the people in south Korea—workers, peasants, soldiers, youth and students, intellectuals and others—must rise up bravely in the save-the-nation struggle against the U.S. imperialist aggressors. The south Korean people must fight against the U.S. imperialist policy of aggression and war and determinedly reject any cooperation with the invader army. The south Korean people should put an end to the outrages committed by U.S. troops against our compatriots, our brothers and sisters, and wage a decisive struggle to force the aggressors out of our territory.

The south Korean people must fight both U.S. imperialism and the internal reactionary forces conspiring with it.

Under the banner of independent, peaceful reunification, the

44 KIM IL SUNG

workers and peasants and all the patriotic, democratic forces of south Korea must form a broad united front for national salvation against U.S. imperialism; they must completely isolate the U.S. imperialists and the internal reactionary forces and prevent the reactionary rulers from relying on outside forces by constantly bringing pressure to bear on them.

We are living in a great era of national-liberation revolutions, when all the oppressed nations of the world are valiantly rising up to win their freedom and independence, casting aside the fetters of imperialism and colonialism. The spirit of struggle for national liberation is running high today in Asia, Africa and Latin America.

In such an era, how could our wise and courageous nation, which has a long history and culture of thousands of years and which has inherited the glorious revolutionary traditions, succumb to the oppression of Yankee imperialism and tolerate colonial slavery? All of us should rise up vigorously and intensify the flames of struggle for the reunification of the nation and the complete independence of the country, fighting U.S. imperialism and its accomplices, the reactionary ruling forces.

When the whole nation is firmly united and fighting a vigorous anti-U.S. save-the-nation struggle, the U.S. imperialist aggressors will finally be driven out of south Korea and the great task of national reunification will certainly be accomplished.

Reply to the Letter of the President of the Korean Affairs Institute in Washington

January 8, 1965

I have received your letter. It gives me great pleasure to learn that you are deeply concerned about the question of reunifying the country.

As you know, our nation has been a victim of territorial partition and national division for 20 years.

Although a new generation has grown up, there has not even been established contact and travel between north and south Korea, to say nothing of the reunification of the country, the long-cherished aspiration of the nation. The artificial barrier of national partition remains unchanged.

As the days go by, the gap between the north and south is growing wider in all spheres of political, economic and cultural life, and even the national characteristics common to our people, a homogeneous nation formed through a long history, are gradually becoming differentiated.

The division of the nation rules out the possibility of coordinated mobilization and use of the national wealth and the strength of the people for the development of the country; it brings unbearable suffering to all Korean people.

The division of Korea into north and south brings immeasurable miseries and misfortunes, particularly to the people living in south Korea.

The prosperity of the whole nation cannot be expected and the people in south Korea cannot be rescued from their wretched plight unless the division of our country is terminated and reunification is achieved.

It is natural that in south Korea today, the broad masses of the people are crying out that they cannot live unless the country is reunified and many public figures with national conscience are fighting courageously for the reunification of the country.

Reunification of the country is an urgent national task which cannot be postponed any longer.

It is high time, we believe, for all Koreans without exception, who are patriotic and concerned about the future of the nation, to do their utmost to reunify the country.

The whole world knows that our Government, expressing the universal desire and will of the entire Korean people, has made persevering efforts to achieve the reunification of the country.

We consider that the solution of the reunification question must not be obstructed by the interests of any party, grouping or privileged circle at the expense of the national interests, and that reunification must in any case be accomplished in a democratic way, in accordance with the general will of the entire Korean people, and not by one side forcing its will on the other side. We do not allow anyone to impose their will upon us, and we, on our part, do not intend to force our will on others. We have always maintained that the authorities, political parties, social organizations and individual personalities of north and south Korea should sit down together and negotiate sincerely and open-heartedly to solve the question of reunification.

I make it clear once again that, just as we have done up to now, so in the future as well, our Government will exert every effort to achieve the reunification of the country in conformity with the desire of the people and the national interests, and that it is ready to accept anyone's opinion, if it is helpful toward the solution of the reunification question.

In your letter you set forth views that have many points in

common with a number of proposals we have already made time and again for the settlement of the question of reunifying the country.

As we have always maintained, the reunification of the country must be carried out in accord with the principles of independence and democracy, and in a peaceful way, without the interference of any outside forces.

We consider that any attempt to reunify the country by relying on outside forces is nothing but an illusion and is designed to leave the whole of Korea in the hands of the imperialist aggressors.

The question of Korean reunification is an internal affair of the Korean people which admits no interference from outside forces. The Korean question must be settled by the Koreans themselves. Foreigners are not in a position to solve the internal affairs of our nation.

Ours is a resourceful and civilized nation, fully capable of solving its nation problem by itself.

The basic obstacle to the country's reunification is the U.S. imperialists who are occupying south Korea militarily, interfering in our domestic affairs, carrying out a policy of dividing our nation, and pursuing an aggressive policy against the whole of Korea.

The U.S. imperialists have brought south Korea completely under their colonial domination in all political, economic, military and cultural fields and brought utter ruin to the life of its people.

Withdrawal of all foreign troops from south Korea is the prerequisite to the solution of the question of reunification.

In north Korea there are absolutely no foreign troops. The Chinese People's Volunteers withdrew completely from north Korea on their own initiative as early as 1958.

However, the U.S. Army in the guise of the United Nations is stationed in south Korea.

The United States has no ground or excuse whatsoever to station its army in south Korea.

There can be no independence or sovereignty as long as a foreign army of aggression is stationed on one's territory.

Any people who have the least spark of national conscience ought to demand the withdrawal of the U.S. troops and work to expel them from our territory.

We must stir up the indignation of the entire nation against the U.S. imperialist aggressors and mobilize all the patriotic forces in the struggle to drive the U.S. army out of south Korea.

Your proposal that all foreign troops should be withdrawn in order to solve the question of Korean reunification is a just one.

It is our consistent view that the question of Korean reunification should be solved through the establishment of a unified central government embracing representatives of people of all classes and strata, through free north-south general elections to be held in a democratic way, without interference by any outside forces, after the withdrawal of all foreign troops from south Korea.

Such general elections should be held in a completely free and democratic atmosphere, without any conditions that might hamper or repress, even slightly, the expression of the will of the people. Free, democratic elections are inconceivable as long as the democratic rights of the people are being violated and patriotic movements suppressed.

To hold free north-south general elections, there should first be full guarantees of complete freedom of political activity for all the political parties, social organizations and individual personalities, as well as freedom of speech, the press, assembly, association and demonstration, throughout north and south Korea. All the political prisoners who have been arrested and imprisoned for having demanded democratic liberties and the country's independent reunification should be set free unconditionally.

All citizens should have equal rights to elect and to be elected at any place throughout Korea, regardless of party affiliation, political views, property status, education, religious faith or sex.

Only through such genuinely democratic elections based on the principles of universal, equal and direct suffrage by secret ballot, can a unified independent and democratic government be established which represents the interests of the workers, peasants, youth and students, intellectuals, servicemen, traders, entrepreneurs and others from all classes and strata.

This proposal of ours is most fair and reasonable, acceptable to everyone.

However, the successive rulers of south Korea have doggedly opposed our just proposal, and have clamored for the so-called "elections under UN supervision."

The Korean people know only too well what "elections under UN supervision" are. It is no secret that the election of Syngman Rhee, traitor to the Korean people, was rigged up more than once, that Chang Myon's assumption to power was fabricated and the seizure of power by Pak Jung Hi was legalized, all through "elections under UN supervision" imposed on south Korea from 1948 to this date.

"Elections under UN supervision" are no more than a screen for covering the insidious aggressive plot of the U.S. imperialists to extend to north Korea the colonial system which they have forced upon the people in south Korea.

In Korea the United Nations has been used as an aggressive tool of the United States.

The United Nations has no competence whatsoever to involve itself in the Korean question.

The Korean people do not want anyone meddling in the solution of the question of their country's reunification. We must in any case achieve the reunification of the country by ourselves.

As the south Korean rulers, at the instigation of U.S. imperialism, persisted in opposing the establishment of a unified government of Korea through free, democratic elections, we could not merely sit with folded arms waiting for the day of reunification and could not but seek ways of gradual approach to complete reunification by taking all steps conducive to the reunification of the country.

You must know that we have long since been proposing the establishment of a Confederation of north and south Korea as a transitional step for settling the urgent and immediate problems of the nation even before the attainment of complete reunification of the country, and for facilitating reunification.

The Confederation we have proposed envisages the formation of a Supreme National Committee composed of equal numbers of representatives appointed by the two governments, mainly with the object of coordinating the economic and cultural development of north and south Korea in a unified way and of promoting mutual cooperation and exchange between the two sides in the common interests of the nation, while retaining the existing political systems in north and south Korea and maintaining the independent activities of the two governments.

The reunification commission you have suggested can be regarded as analogous to the Supreme National Committee we have mentioned. In our opinion, it would also be a good idea to work out measures for restoring the national bonds between the north and south and for carrying out the reunification of the country independently, not necessarily through the form of a Confederation, but by setting up some other kind of joint organ to be composed of representatives from north and south Korea.

We have maintained time and again that if the south Korean authorities cannot accept the Confederation, then the nation's tribulations caused by the division should at least be softened by effecting north-south economic and cultural exchange, leaving aside political questions for the time being.

The economic exchange between the north and the south would organically combine industrial north Korea with agrarian south Korea and facilitate the unified, independent development of the national economy, and would open the way for reviving south Korea's ruined economy and stabilizing the living conditions of its people who are in dire straits.

We have already built a developed industry and agriculture and laid firm economic foundations for an independent state in north Korea. This is the economic asset which would permit our nation to live independently after the country is reunified in the future.

When we were rebuilding, with tightened belts, the economy that had been ravaged beyond description by the U.S. imperialist aggressors, we were always mindful of the interests and future development of the whole nation. We have not for a moment forgotten our compatriots in south Korea; we consider it our sacred national duty to help the suffering people in south Korea.

Along with the carrying out of economic exchange, cultural ties in all spheres of science, culture, arts, sports, etc., should be restored, and travel of people between north and south should be effected.

The south Korean authorities, following the dictates of U.S. imperialism, are opposed to free north-south general elections, opposed to a Confederation of north and south Korea and opposed even to economic and cultural exchange and travel of people between north and south.

Under these circumstances, we insist that at least the exchange of letters should be materialized as a minimum step for forging ties between the north and south. This reflects the pressing demand of the people for ending the extremely abnormal situation in which parents, wives and children, relatives and friends who are separated in the north and the south cannot even write to each other.

It is of prime importance in achieving the reunification of the country to eliminate the tension created between the north and the south.

In this connection, it might be recalled, we have time and again proposed to the south Korean authorities that, after U.S. troops are completely withdrawn from south Korea, north and south Korean authorities conclude a peace agreement pledging not to resort to armed attack against each other, and that the armed forces of both north and south Korea be reduced to 100,000 or less.

The oversize armed forces of south Korea, numbering more than 600,000 men, are an unbearably heavy military expenditure for the south Korean people and severely menace peace in Korea.

The withdrawal of all foreign troops from south Korea, the conclusion of a peace agreement between the north and the south and the reduction of the armed forces on both sides will mark a giant step forward on the road to the country's reunification.

We regard as a welcome idea your proposal that the north and south Korean armies be cut to the level of constabulary units for the maintenance of internal security and order.

We are ready to take any other steps that may be helpful to the solution of the reunification question. We are willing to abrogate the military pacts we have concluded with foreign countries on the condition that the U.S. army is withdrawn from south Korea and the south Korean authorities abolish all the military pacts and agreements they have signed with foreign countries. We made this clear previously, when we were concluding the pacts with other countries.

Ours is an independent people's power established freely in accordance with the general will of the people. We have never relied on outside forces; we maintain complete independence in all spheres—political, economic, military and cultural.

Our domestic and foreign policies are completely independent, brooking no interference from any foreign country. Our Government, whenever it deems it necessary for the interests of the country and the nation, can take appropriate actions on its own initiative.

We have devoted all our sincere efforts to the reunification of our country.

Even after the present rulers of south Korea staged a military coup and seized power, we repeatedly advanced a number of proposals of national salvation aimed at removing the national calamity and accelerating the reunification of the country, in the sincere hope that they would return to a national position. However, following the aggressive and the divisive policy of the U.S. imperialists and disregarding the ardent desire of the nation, they have refused to listen to our sincere advice; on the contrary, they continue to perpetuate the partition of the nation.

The responsibility for the failure up to now to achieve the reunification of our country rests with the U.S. imperialists who have occupied south Korea by force of arms and have been pursuing a policy of splitting our nation, and with such traitors as Pak Jung Hi, the reactionary bureaucrats, the political quacks and impostors who, hand in glove with the U.S. imperialists, are bartering away the interests of the nation.

They serve the foreign aggressive forces, opposing the independent and peaceful reunification of the country and categorically rejecting the unity of the national forces; they defend only their own personal interests and those of some privileged circles that are in league with outside forces; they can never represent the south Korean people.

They defend, and ask for the permanent stationing of, the U.S. aggressive army which has occupied south Korea and has been obstructing the reunification of our country and perpetrating all and every kind of brutish atrocity such as plundering, oppressing, insulting and killing people in south Korea.

Those traitors, turning down our offer to receive millions of unemployed south Koreans into north Korea and give them jobs, are selling out our compatriots to European and American countries as if they were commodities.

Moreover, they are even ushering in the Japanese militarists to reduce south Korea to a colony of both U.S. and Japanese imperialism.

Manipulated by the United States, the traitors of south Korea, dead set against contact and cooperation within one and the same nation, are hurrying through the criminal "ROK-Japan talks" for collusion with the Japanese militarists.

Those taking the lead in conspiring with Japanese imperialism are the same stooges who served it faithfully in the past, too. Refusing to repent of their past crimes, they have now again become the cat's paw of U.S. imperialism and their old master, Japanese militarism.

To achieve the reunification of the country, we should pool the strength of the entire Korean people in north and south and fight against the foreign imperialist aggressive forces and their allies—the traitors, reactionary bureacrats, political quacks and impostors who are hindering reunification.

How can we promote national unity and achieve the reunification of the country without fighting against those who, far from desiring reunification, categorically reject any contact or exchange between the north and south?

Needless to say, it would be a different matter if even now they were to repent of their mistakes and take the road of struggle for the withdrawal of the U.S. army and for the independent reunification of the country.

If a man defends the interests of the nation and desires the country's reunification, we will join hands and go together with him at any time, regardless of his political views and ideology and of his past record.

If all the patriotic forces of north and south Korea unite, we will definitely open the road to contact and negotiation between the north and the south, realize mutual cooperation and exchange, force the U.S. army to withdraw, and achieve the reunification of the country.

Without unity and struggle we can neither drive out the U.S. aggressor army nor achieve national reunification.

The point is that the south Korean people of all walks of life—workers, peasants, youth and students, intellectuals, armymen, traders, entrepreneurs, etc.—should firmly unite and wage a more resolute national-salvation struggle against U.S. imperialism and its stooges, for the independent and peaceful reunification of the country.

We should under no circumstances tolerate any form of interference in the domestic affairs of our nation; we must thoroughly oppose "protection" or "supervision" by anyone and must carve out our own destiny by ourselves.

When we achieve the reunification of our country on the principle of the self-determination of nations and when the whole nation fights in unity, we will be able to increase the might of the country and build a rich and powerful, independent sovereign state, without needing "guarantees" from any outside forces.

Our country will surely be reunified through the nationwide struggle of the entire Korean people.

In conclusion, I express the hope that you will make positive efforts to accelerate the independent reunification of the country.

Let us Embody the Revolutionary Spirit of Independence, Self-sustenance and Self-defense More Thoroughly in all Fields of State Activity [Excerpt]

Political program of the Government of the Democratic People's Republic of Korea Announced at the First Session of the Fourth Supreme People's Assembly of the DPRK, December 16, 1967

First. The Government of the Republic will thoroughly implement the line of independence, self-sustenance and self-defense to consolidate the political independence of the country, further strengthen the foundations of an independent national economy capable of ensuring the complete reunification, independence and prosperity of our nation, and increase the defense capabilities of the country so as to reliably safeguard its security on the basis of our own forces, by excellently materializing our Party's idea of *Juche* in all fields.

Our Party's idea of *Juche* represents the most correct Marxist-Leninist idea of leadership for the successful accomplishment of our revolution and construction and is the invariable guiding principle of the Government of the Republic in all its policies and activities.

Only by firmly establishing *Juche* can each country repudiate flunkyism to great powers and dogmatism and creatively apply the universal truth of Marxism-Leninism and the experience of other countries in line with its historical conditions and national characteristics; always solve its own problems by itself on its own responsibility, eliminating reliance on others while displaying the spirit of self-reliance; and, accordingly, carry on its revolutionary cause and construction work successfully.

Establishing *Juche* is a question of special importance for us in the light of our country's geographical situation and environment, the specifics of its historical development and the complex and arduous character of our revolution. The establishment of *Juche* is a question of key importance on which the success of our revolution depends, a vital question which will determine the future of our nation.

The Government of the Republic has been able to score great victories and successes in the revolutionary struggle and construction work, as it has persistently endeavored to solve all problems independently, in conformity with the specific realities of our country and mainly through its own efforts, guided consistently by the *Juche* idea of the Workers' Party of Korea in its activities and strictly adhering to the principles of Marxism-Leninism.

As a result of our efforts to establish *Juche* in the ideological field, the national pride of our workers and their sense of independence have grown tremendously, and they have acquired these revolutionary characteristics: not following others blindly, approaching foreign things critically instead of mechanically copying or swallowing them whole; and striving to solve all problems according to the actual conditions of our country and on the basis of their own wisdom and strength.

Thanks to the fact that our Party's spirit of independence, self-sustenance and self-defense is finding full expression in all fields of national construction, the political independence of the Republic has been consolidated and the economic independence and military power of our country have grown even more.

As a full-fledged, independent state, our country now sets its own lines and policies independently and exercises complete equality and sovereignty in its foreign relations.

Under the leadership of our Party and the Government of the

Republic, our people have laid firm foundations for an independent national economy in accord with the revolutionary principle of self-reliance and thus eliminated the centuries-old backwardness and poverty, further increased the economic might of the Republic and radically imporved their standard of living. The estblishment of *Juche* in science and culture has accelerated scientific and technological progress, brought about a great qualitative change in education and in the work of training cadres, and led to the blossoming and advancement of a new, socialist national culture congenial to the life and sentiments of our people.

In the field of defense construction, too, we have strengthened our defense capabilities to such an extent that we are in a position to firmly defend the security of our country and our socialist gains, even in the complex situation existing today, on the basis of our own strength.

The great victories and successes we have attained in our socialist revolution and socialist construction over the past years are, indeed, the brilliant fruition of the great vitality of our Party's idea of *Juche* and of our line of independence, self-sustenance and self-defense—the embodiment of that idea in all fields. We formulated our policies independently by creatively applying the principles of Marxism-Leninism to the specific realities of Korea and enlisted the inexhaustible creative potential of our industrious and talented people and our rich national resources to carry out these policies. This has enabled us to build a socialist state in a short time, which has political independence, economic self-sustenance and national self-defense.

Our Party's line of strengthening the political, economic and military might of the country in every way with all our efforts is the most correct way of expediting the victory of the Korean revolution.

The Government of the Republic will continue to adhere firmly to the principle of settling independently all the problems that arise in revolution and construction, studying and analyzing the realities of Korea in strict accordance with the *Juche* idea of the Workers' Party of Korea.

All nations are equal and have the solemn right of national self-determination, of deciding their own destinies for themselves. A nation can secure independence and freedom and attain welfare and prosperity only if it achieves complete political self-determination and exercises its rights, taking them firmly into its hands.

Under the leadership of our Party, the Government of the Republic will use its own head in formulating all our policies for socialist construction in the fields of industry, agriculture, education, literature and art, judicial administration, etc., in conformity with our realities, and carry them out with its own efforts. We must not act on orders and instructions of others but, on the basis of the interests of our revolution and construction, settle all problems from the standpoint of *Juche*, using our own judgment and making our own decisions. It is true that we should unite with friends who are fighting for a common goal and learn from their experience if it accords with the principles of Marxism-Leninism, and it is worth learning. But even so, we must always approach such experience critically, vehemently opposing the tendency to swallow foreign things whole or imitate them mechanically; we must not blindly copy what does not fit our actual conditions.

In the struggle for our country's reunification, too, the Government of the Republic will always hold fast to its independent position. We regard all attempts to effect the country's reunification by relying on outside forces as treacheries against the country and the nation, aimed at placing the whole of Korea in the hands of foreign aggressors. The question of Korean reunification is an internal affair of the Korean people, one which cannot be settled by any outside forces. Ours is a wise and civilized nation, fully capable of settling its national problems for itself. We consistently hold that the question of reunifying our country must be settled through the efforts of our people themselves, without interference from any outside forces, under the condition that the aggressive army of U.S. imperialism is withdrawn from south Korea.

In the sphere of foreign policy, too, we should continue to work to establish political and economic relations with other countries on the principles of complete equality and mutual respect. We must always rely on our own judgment and conviction in struggling against imperialism and Right and "Left" opportunism, in conformity with our actual conditions, and let no one violate and affront the rights and dignity of our nation.

The Government of the Republic will continue to faithfully carry out our Party's line of building an independent national economy by fully applying the principle of self-reliance in the economic sphere, while, at the same time, consolidating political independence.

Today we are confronted with the weighty task of carrying on economic construction and defense upbuilding in parallel, to lay a firm material foundation for the prosperity of all the generations to come and establish a sound economic base which will enable us to readily cope with the great revolutionary event of the reunification of our country. All this can be achieved successfully only if the principle of self-reliance, the line of building an independent national economy is adhered to consistently and implemented more thoroughly.

Self-reliance is a thoroughly revolutionary stand for a people to accomplish the revolution in their country mainly relying on their own forces; it is an independent stand of building up their country through their own labor and with their own national resources.

Only by firmly maintaining such a revolutionary stand and revolutionary principle can we carry on the struggle without forsaking revolutionary constancy, no matter what complex and difficult situation may confront us, and assure victory in the revolutionary struggle and success in our work of construction, bravely overcoming difficulties and hardships that stand in the way of our advance. If you lack the revolutionary spirit of self-reliance, you may lose faith in your own strength, neglect efforts to tap the inner resources of your country, grow indolent and loose, and fall into a state of passivity and conservatism.

Only when a nation builds an independent national economy can it secure political independence, make its country rich, strong and advanced, and achieve national prosperity.

Economic independence is the material foundation for political independence. A country which is economically dependent on outside forces becomes a political satellite of other countries; an economically subjected nation cannot free itself from colonial slavery politically.

Without building an independent national economy it is impossible to establish material and technological foundations for socialism, and build socialism and communism successfully.

To build socialism, it is essential to create a powerful base of heavy industry with the machine-building industry as its core, and, on this basis, equip light industry, agriculture, transport and all other branches of the national economy with up-to-date techniques, thus laying the powerful material and technological foundations for socialism—needed to improve the welfare of the working people as a whole—as the laws of socialism require.

As long as national distinctions remain and states exist, these material and technological foundations of socialism must be built by each national state as a unit. Therefore, it can be said that firm material and technological foundations of socialism have been laid in each country only when it has built a comprehensive, independent national economy diversified in its development, equipped with the latest technology and run by its own national cadres, using its own natural resources, raw materials and other supplies so that its domestic products can fully meet the varied and ever-growing requirements of economic and defense construction and the people's consumption, for heavy and light industrial goods and farm produce.

Only if the material and technological foundations of socialism are established in this way within the bounds of each national state as a comprehensive, independent economic unit, can the country's natural resources be tapped and utilized to the fullest and a high rate of growth in production be maintained together with a correct and flexible balance among all branches of the national economy. Moreover, only in this way is it possible to develop science, technology and culture rapidly, steadily raise the technological and cultural standards of the working people, and turn them into people of a new type, developed in an all-round way.

The building of an independent national economy is also the

basic guarantee that nations can eliminate the economic back-wardness which constitutes the real basis of inequalities be-tween them, achieve national prosperity and build a socialist and communist society successfully.

The building of a socialism and communism, as you know, requires the eradication of inequalities between nations as well as of class distinctions.

Such inequalities, however, do not disappear immediately when the socialist revolution triumphs in each country, nor do they vanish through the amalgamation of nations in one way or another.

The era of capitalism is an era in which national oppression prevails side by side with class exploitation, an era in which the free development of the great majority of nations is held back by a few nations and inequalities between nations exist. It is, there-fore, necessary for the nations liberated from capitalist exploita-tion and oppression not only to become laboring socialist na-tions but also to build highly developed, independent national economies for their fullest free development and all-round efflorescence. Only by so doing can all inequalities among nations be done away with and can all nations build socialism with success, and gradually go on to communism.

All this testifies to the fact that the line of building an inde-pendent national economy, consistently followed by our Party and the Government of the Republic, is a thoroughly revolu-tionary line of economic construction that conforms with the laws which govern the building of socialism and communism.

We will apply the revolutionary principle of self-reliance in building up our national defenses as well, and thus further increase our country's capabilities for self-defense.

Needless to say, the international unity of the proletariat of all countries and the friendly alliance of the socialist countries in the revolutionary struggle against imperialist aggression and against the pressures of international capital are an important guarantee for safeguarding the revolutionary gains already obtained and winning new victories. It is the sacred inter-nationalist duty of Communists to do all they can to help and give support and encouragement to each other in the battle against imperialism, their common enemy, and each country should strive to strengthen this international solidarity in the struggle against imperialist forces of aggression from without.

The decisive factor for victory in the struggle against imperialist reaction, however, is the internal forces of the country concerned. Although foreign support is important in a war against foreign aggressors, to all intents and purposes it plays no more than a secondary role. When the internal forces in a country are not prepared, its revolutionary struggle cannot emerge victorious, no matter how great its foreign support may be. If the Communists only pin their hopes on foreign support and aid, without developing their own revolutionary forces, they cannot be sure of defending the security of their country and their revolutionary gains against imperialist aggression.

The Government of the Republic will materialize our Party's spirit of self-defense, thoroughly preparing our people and soldiers politically and ideologically for war; it will make full material preparations to defend our country, relying on the solid foundations of the independent national economy we have already established and, at the same time, further increase our military might.

Particularly, by carrying out the decisions of the Conference of the Workers' Party of Korea in full, we will concentrate all our efforts on reorganizing the whole work of building our socialist economy to fit the requirements of the present situations and on reinforcing our defense capabilities to meet the undisguised aggressive maneuvers by the enemy. Thus we will make ours an ever more solid and viable, independent economy to fully meet the material needs of both the front lines and the rear in case of emergency, and we will make our country's military power impregnable to repel the enemy on our own no matter when he may launch a surprise attack against us.

Materializing the *Juche* idea of the Workers' Party of Korea successfully in all fields, we will build an ever richer, stronger and mightier socialist state—independent in politics, self-sustaining in the economy and self-defensive in national defense.

Second. In order to end the present misfortunes of our people caused by the artificial split of our territory and nation as soon as possible, liberate the people in south Korea and reunify our country, the Government of the Republic will firmly equip the people in the northern half morally and materially to always support the south Korean people in their sacred anti-U.S. struggle for national salvation and to readily cope with the great revolutionary event.

Because of the occupation of south Korea by the U.S. imperialists, our country is still divided into north and south, and the reunification of the country, the heartfelt desire of the nation has not yet been achieved even though a new generation has grown up. Our people have been suffering from the national split for more than 20 years. As the days go by, the gulf between north and south Korea is widening in all spheres —political, economic and cultural—and the national community of our people, formed through a long history, is gradually melting away. Territorial partition and national split make it impossible to coordinate our efforts to enlist and utilize our country's wealth and national wisdom and talents to promote the prosperity of the country and the welfare of the people.

The division of Korea into north and south has caused immeasurable misery and distress particularly to the south Korean people. South Korea today has been completely turned into a colony of U.S. imperialists, into their military base of aggression. The national industry of south Korea has been reduced to dependency on foreign capital, and its agriculture, too, is in serious crisis. The national culture and the beautiful customs inherent in the Korean people have been utterly trampled underfoot, and all kinds of immorality and depravity prevail everywhere in south Korea. The south Korean people are going hungry, in rags, doubly and triply exploited and oppressed, many of them roaming the streets in quest of work and living in a state of constant anxiety with all hopes blighted. They are subjected to unbearable racial insults and contempt, and even their right to existence is constantly threatened by the U.S. imperialist aggressors.

Where there are exploitation and oppression, there will always be revolutionary struggle on the part of the people. Ever since the first days of the occupation of the southern half by the U.S. imperialist aggressors, the south Korean people have been fighting tenaciously against their policies of colonial enslavement and military aggression. The October Popular Resistance Struggle in 1946, the April Uprising in 1960 which toppled the puppet regime of Syngman Rhee, and many struggles waged successively by the south Korean people against the "ROK-Japan talks" and for the abrogation of the "ROK-Japan agreements," dealt telling blows to the colonial rule of U.S. imperialism.

Each time, the U.S. imperialists and their stooges harshly repressed the people's righteous patriotic struggle at the point of the bayonet. The policy of military fascist dictatorship pursued in south Korea today has assumed unprecedented ferocity and barbarity and has become a prototype of vicious fascist rule by the imperialists over their colonies. The U.S. imperialist aggressors and their puppets, while manufacturing numerous wicked fascist laws, greatly increased their repressive apparatus, and covered the whole of south Korea with military, police, intelligence and special agent networks, thereby turning it into a living hell of terrorism and murder.

In south Korea today the U.S. imperialists and the Pak Jung Hi clique are intensifying their fascist repression to the limit. Everywhere they are making all sorts of frenzied attempts to repress the south Korean people, who are fighting harder than ever for the right to live, for democratic liberties and for the reunification of their country. According to south Korean press reports, this year alone ten or more divisions including U.S. imperialist troops, south Korean puppet army, police forces, and reserve divisions, were mobilized to crush the actions of armed groups of south Korean revolutionaries and the mass revolutionary struggles, breaking out one after another all over south Korea. A total of more than six million U.S. imperialist troops, south Korean puppet troops and police took part directly in the so-called "mopping-up operations." The U.S. imperialists and the Pak Jung Hi clique cruelly suppressed the revolutionary organization formed around Dr. Kim Dae Su, professor at Kyongbuk University, arresting and imprisoning more than ten patriotic intellectuals. Last autumn they arrested many young people in and around Pusan on the charge of involvement in the alleged case of the People's Revolutionary Party. Again, they recently used trumped-up charges in what they called the "case of the Operative Group for the Communization of South Korea" in Seoul and, on the other hand, arrested and imprisoned many university professors, other intellectuals and patriotic figures, branding the Society for Comparative Studies on Nationalism —an academic organization—as a "seditious organization," and tried the victims in a kangaroo court. They have thus committed the heinous crime of "demanding" the death penalty or life imprisonment for many innocent persons.

They are raising an ever louder "anti-communist" hue and cry under the nonsensical allegation that all the fierce revolutionary struggles of the patriotic people which are breaking out all over south Korea today are the work of "spies" sent down from north Korea; and they are trying hard to take the minds of the south Korean people off their troubles and to deceive the peoples of the world.

But no amount of brutal repression and "anti-communist" campaign by the U.S. imperialists and the Pak Jung Hi puppet clique can ever dampen the indomitable revolutionary fighting spirit of the south Korean people or block their sweeping revolutionary advance. Today broad sections of the south Korean people are waging a vigorous struggle in all fields, holding still higher the banner of anti-U.S. resistance struggle for national salvation. A people can win freedom and liberation only through its own struggle. When the broad masses of the people rise as one in a struggle against their oppressors, they can destroy any imperialist bulwark. If the workers and peasants, youth and students, intellectuals and other broad sectors of the people in south Korea unite firmly and come out courageously in revolutionary struggle, they will be able to deal a crushing defeat to the U.S. imperialists and the Pak Jung Hi clique and accomplish the cause of the south Korean revolution.

On behalf of the entire people in the northern half of the Republic, I send warm revolutionary greetings to the revolutionaries and democratic figures, to all the patriotic people who are putting up a valiant struggle in various parts of south Korea, underground, in mountains, and even in prison.

All the people in the northern half of the Republic bear the great responsibility of carrying the south Korean revolution to a conclusion, giving active support to the struggle of the south Korean people, keeping up with their exalted fighting spirit.

As long as the U.S. imperialists continue to occupy south Korea and our country remains partitioned, the Korean people cannot live in peace even for a moment and the people in south Korea cannot extricate themselves from their present misery and pain. The occupation of south Korea by U.S. imperialism and its policy of aggression are the source of all the misfortunes of our nation and the main obstacle to the reunification of our country.

We cannot simply contemplate the miserable plight of our south Korean compatriots with folded arms and we can never bequeath a divided country to our descendants. As long as this wretched situation continues in which the country and the nation are divided and our compatriots, blood brothers and sisters, are subjected to all sorts of racial insults and ill treatment by the foreign aggressors, no Korean Communist or conscientious Korean nationalist can say that he has fulfilled his duty.

We must accomplish the south Korean revolution and reunify the country in our generation and bequeath a unified country to the new generations. We must prepare all necessary conditions for the reunification of our country as soon as possible.

The acomplishment of the great cause of liberating south Korea and reunifying the country at the earliest possible date depends not only on how the revolutionary organizations and revolutionaries in south Korea expand and strengthen the revolutionary forces and how they fight the enemy but also, to a large extent, on how the people in the northern half of the Republic prepare themselves to cope with the great revolutionary event.

The most important thing in completing the south Korean revolution and hastening the reunification of the country is to well prepare all our people politically and ideologically and, at the same time, create all the necessary material conditions.

We should always give active material and moral support and

encouragement to the south Korean people in their anti-U.S., national-salvation struggle and consider the south Korean revolution and the reunification of the country our first and foremost revolutionary task. We can never allow ourselves to become self-complacent with the achievements wrought in the northern half and become lax and indolent. How can we sit idly by at a time when the south Korean people, suffering from hunger, are waging a struggle at the cost of their blood? It is our lofty national duty and the supreme task of the nation to force the U.S. imperialist aggressors out of our territory, liberate south Korea and reunify our country by pooling our strength with that of the south Korean people.

The people in the northern half of the Republic should always remember their brothers in the south and have revolutionary determination to liberate them at all costs. They should be firmly prepared ideologically to be mobilized for a decisive struggle to accomplish the cause of the reunification of the country by joining forces with the south Korean people whenever called upon to go to their aid, as the struggle of the people surges forward and the revolutionary situation ripens in south Korea.

Meanwhile, socialist economic construction, the principal guarantee for strengthening the material forces of our revolutionary base, should be successfully carried on to further consolidate the economic foundations of our country so that adequate material preparations can be made to support the revolutionary struggle of the south Korean people and to readily cope with the great revolutionary event of realizing the reunification of our country.

The present situation requires us to conduct all our work in a more active, more revolutionary manner. We must subordinate everything to the struggle to accomplish the south Korean revolution by giving support to the south Korean people in their struggle and to reunify our country.

The northern half of the Republic is the revolutionary base for accomplishing the great cause of national liberation throughout the country, and its revolutionary forces are the most important motive power for the Korean revolution as a whole. All the working people should fully realize that, unless the revolutionary base of the northern half of the Republic is fortified and its revolutionary forces are strengthened still more, it will be impossible to give positive support to the south Korean revolution and achieve the reunification of our country. They must continue to wage a tenacious struggle on all fronts of the socialist economic construction and produce and build more, better and cheaper with our existing manpower, equipment and materials by discovering and activating reserves and potentialities to the utmost. All functionaries and working people, as masters in their country, should assiduously manage all aspects of economic life, both national and individual, and make every effort not to waste a single grain of rice, a single gram of iron or a single drop of gasoline.

Only when our country's economic foundations are more consolidated and the necessary material conditions are sufficiently created can we cope with the great event with full preparations, bring the superiority of the socialist system home to the fighting people of south Korea and give powerful support to their revolutionary struggle. Only then will it be possible to create assets with which to put the devastated south Korean economy back on its feet and rapidly improve the deteriorated living conditions of the people in the southern half, after the reunification of the country.

All our functionaries and working people should work like masters, and live frugally, with a great revolutionary zeal, in the lofty spirit of supporting the south Korean people more actively in their anti-U.S., national-salvation struggle and of expediting the revolutionary cause of the reunification of the country. We can never get complacent and lax nor countenance the slightest laziness, immorality or luxury. We are making a revolution and we should work and live in a revolutionary way, ready and alert at all times.

All our people will, in this way, be made to readily cope with the great revolutionary event of national reunification. We should all be ready and willing to take part in the revolutionary struggle whenever called upon to do so by the Party.

Reports to the Fifth Congress of the Workers' Party of Korea on the Work of the Central Committee
[Excerpt]

November 2, 1970

C omrades, the south Korean revolution is a component part of the Korean revolution as a whole. To achieve the victory of the Korean revolution on a nation-wide scale, it is essential to push forcefully ahead with socialist construction in the northern half of the Republic and, at the same time, further advance the revolutionary struggle in south Korea.

The period under review has witnessed tremendous changes in the south Korean situation. The U.S. imperialists have more completely reduced south Korea to a military base of aggression, their military appendage, and pushed their policies of aggression and war harder than ever through a fascist military dictatorship. On the other hand, national and class contradictions have become more acute in south Korea and the revolutionary advance of the workers, peasants and other broad sectors of the people has been stepped up. As a consequence U.S. imperialism's colonial rule has gone into a deeper crisis. These are the main developments which occurred in south Korea over the past period.

The south Korean revolution is a national-liberation revolution against the U.S. imperialist aggressors and, at the same time, a people's democratic revolution against the stooges of U.S. imperialism—the landlords, comprador capitalists and reactionary bureaucrats—and their fascist rule. The basic task of this revolution is to drive the U.S. imperialist forces of aggression out of south Korea, get rid of their colonial domination, and overthrow the fascist military dictatorship in order to establish a progressive social system, thus developing south Korean society democratically.

The U.S. imperialists are the real rulers who have seized all power in south Korea. They are the first target of the south Korean revolutionary struggle. The occupation of south Korea by U.S. imperialism and its colonial rule is the basic cause of all the misery and pains the south Korean people are suffering. Until the U.S. imperialist aggressors are forced out of south Korea and their colonial rule is smashed, the south Korean people cannot escape their present wretched plight. The tiny handful of landlords, comprador capitalists and reactionary bureaucrats in south Korea faithfully execute the aggressive policy of the U.S. imperialists and, under their patronage, cruelly oppress and exploit the people.

The motive power of the south Korean revolution is the working class and its dependable ally, the peasantry, and the progressive student youth, intellectuals, patriotic-minded soldiers and some patriotic national capitalists and petty bourgeoisie who are opposed to U.S. imperialism and its lackeys.

The revolutionary struggle in south Korea is a just struggle of these and other sectors of the people against the U.S. imperialist forces of aggression and their accomplices—the landlords, comprador capitalists and reactionary bureaucrats.

From liberation to the present, the south Korean people have kept up an unflagging revolutionary struggle against U.S. imperialism and its underlings.

The revolutionary struggle of the south Korean people has gradually entered a new stage of development, especially in the postwar years, and hewed its way, despite harsh trials, to greater successes. After the war the south Korean people—inspired by the achievements in socialist revolution and construction in the northern half—fought on staunchly against U.S. imperialism and its stooges, for political freedom, democratic rights and the reunification of the country.

In the course of this struggle, the south Korean revolutionaries and the people have shed much blood and suffered a number of heart-rending setbacks. But their sacrifices and failures have not been in vain. This has gradually made them grasp a valuable truth of revolutionary struggle: the ferocious enemy can be defeated only with an organized force.

The south Korean revolutionaries keenly felt the need to build a party to unite the revolutionary forces into one solid block and to give co-ordinated leadership to the struggle, and they strove to make that materialize. As a result of their untiring struggle and as a reflection of the essential requirements of the development of the south Korean revolutionary movement, the Progressive Party, a legal political party of the south Korean revolutionaries, came into being in December 1955.

The Progressive Party put forward a fighting program with anti-imperialism, anti-fascism and peaceful reunification as its key points and launched an active struggle to rally patriotic democratic forces in various strata, opposing the policies of national division and fascistization pursued by U.S. imperialism and its henchmen. The Progressive Party acquired increased prestige among broad segments of the south Korean people and the peaceful reunification program advanced by the Party especially enjoyed strong support from the south Korean public. This was unquestionably testified during the puppet presidential "election" in 1956, when the Progressive Party "candidate" won more than 2 million votes, or slightly less than what was raked up by Syngman Rhee, loyal ballcarrier for U.S. imperialism—and this despite the outrageous repression, fraud and swindling on the part of U.S. imperialism and its stooges. This graphically showed that the south Korean people were against the fascist colonial rule of U.S. imperialism and its policy of national division and fervently desired the peaceful reunification of our country and democratic social development. The U.S. imperialists and their henchmen were so terrified by the rapidly expanding and increasing influence of the Progressive Party among the south Korean people that they launched bloody repression, perpetrating the bestial barbarity of arresting and imprisoning numerous members of the Progressive Party and slaying its leader Mr. Cho Bong Am. They forcibly dissolved the Party and it ceased to exist in January 1958. Though the Progressive Party failed to transform the fighting spirit of the south Korean people into a mass revolutionary movement against the enemy and even to take effective action to preserve its own revolutionary forces, it gave a considerable impetus to the trend toward national reunification in south Korea and to the development of the anti-U.S., anti-dictatorship struggle of the people.

After the dissolution of the Progressive Party, the U.S. imperialists and their stooges further stepped up their repression of the south Korean patriots. In spite of all hardships and trials, however, the dynamic revolutionary struggle of the people went on without letup and the revolutionary forces grew steadily in south Korea.

The Popular Uprising of April 1960 marked a new turning point in the advancement of the south Korean revolutionary movement. The April Popular Uprising was an explosion of the enmity and resentment of the south Korean people which had long been pent up under the colonial rule of U.S. imperialism and its lackeys. It was a mass resistance struggle against the U.S. and for national salvation, involving millions of the broad masses throughout south Korea. The puppet government of Syngman Rhee, veteran lackey of U.S. imperialism was finally overthrown by the heroic struggle of the masses of the south Korean people, including student youth and intellectuals. This was the first victory won after the war by the south Korean people in their anti-U.S. national-salvation struggle. The April Popular Uprising clearly demonstrated the heroic mettle of the south Korean people and proved that if the masses pool their strength and rise in a struggle against the oppressors, they can certainly crush any enemy stronghold. With the April 19 Uprising the crisis of the colonial rule of U.S. imperialism deepened in south Korea, and the situation turned in favor of the revolution.

Following the April Popular Uprising, the revolutionary advance of the patriots and the masses of south Korea intensified with each passing day and progressive political forces appeared on the scene. In this process the Socialist Mass Party came into being. Under the guidance of the south Korean revolutionaries the Socialist Mass Party set forth, as its immediate task, the founding of a unified democratic state based on the line of national independence, and conducted brisk organizational and political activities aimed at leading a massive advance of the people in a national-salvation movement for the independent reunification of our country. The Party formed the "Central Council for Independent National Reunification," a united-front coalition of the broad democratic forces, and organized and directed the joint struggle of all strata of the people against U.S. imperialism and its lackeys. Under the leadership of the Socialist Mass Party the fierce flames of struggle enveloped the whole of south Korea. The student youth and people there waged a heroic fight to tear down the barrier between north and south, with slogans like "Reunification is the only way out," "Let's go north, come south, let's meet at Panmunjom!"

The Socialist Mass Party, however, was not able to develop the revolutionary advance of the student youth into a struggle that would end the occupation of south Korea by U.S. imperialism, smash its colonial ruling machine and establish a democratic government; nor could it organize the workers, peasants and other sectors of the broad masses, and mobilize them in the struggle. When the U.S. imperialists instigated the reactionary military gangsters to stage a counterrevolutionary "military coup" and make a fascist attack on the revolutionary forces, the Socialist Mass Party failed to deal a resolute counterstroke, and in the end the struggle of the students was suppressed.

After the May 16 "military coup" the U.S. imperialists and their stooges launched into naked fascist military rule in south Korea. They trampled on even the elementary democratic freedoms and rights of the south Korean people and forcibly dissolved all progressive political parties and social organizations, closed down organs of the press and perpetrated such barbarities as the wholesale arrest, imprisonment and slaughter of hundreds of thousands of revolutionaries and patriotic people. The Socialist Mass Party was thus destroyed by brutal repression on the part of the enemy, and the revolutionary forces of south Korea suffered heavy losses.

But the revolutionaries and patriotic people of south Korea were further awakened and acquired many valuable lessons and precious experience in this postwar process of struggle. The historical experience of the south Korean revolutionary movement has clearly proven that there can be no peaceful transition in the struggle for power and that no revolution can be led to victory by a mass movement alone. Under the patronage of U.S. imperialism, the successive reactionary rulers of south Korea cold-bloodedly slaughtered progressive figures backed by the people when there appeared even the slightest likelihood of their assumption of power. Every mass movement of the people for national reunification against U.S. imperialist colonial rule was answered with barbarous repression. The Progressive Party was crushed as soon as it gained popularity in the elections with its slogan of national reunification, and the Socialist Mass Party was also forcibly dissolved when it led the broad masses in the national-salvation struggle for the reunification of our country and won high prestige among the people. It is usual for the enemy to resort to terrorism against those who are inclined to take a revolutionary stand for the sake of their country and nation. Shortly after liberation, the enemy assassinated Mr. Ryo Un Hyong simply because he had advocated the peaceful reunification of the country. They also assassinated Mr. Kim Gu when he turned progressive after attending the Joint Conference of Representatives of the North and South Korean Political Parties and Social Organizations. The revolutionaries and patriotic people in south Korea came to realize more keenly that they could win power only through revolutionary struggle, since the reactionary south Korean rulers would not meekly relinquish their ruling power but were desperately resorting to counterrevolutionary violence to stifle the progressive forces. They drew from this the priceless lesson that, in order to win victory for the revolution, they had to be fully prepared to resist the enemy's counterrevolutionary violence with revolutionary violence, while waging an active mass struggle for democratization against fascism.

The April 19 Popular Uprising and subsequent developments, in particular, taught an important lesson: that the people could win their democratic freedoms and rights only through a decisive revolutionary struggle to drive the U.S. imperialist aggressors out of south Korea and overthrow the colonial rule of U.S. imperialism and that this struggle would emerge victorious only when the broad masses of the people, including workers, peasants and student youth, were mobilized under the leadership of a Marxist-Leninist Party, the vanguard detachment of the working class.

Drawing on the valuable experiences and lessons acquired at the cost of blood in their struggle against the enemy, the south Korean revolutionaries have devoted their all to developing the revolutionary struggle in defiance of cruel repression by the fascist military rulers. In the establishment of a Marxist-Leninist Party of the working class they found the key to overcoming the most serious weaknesses of the previous revolutionary movements in south Korea and to advancing the revolution successfully. They hastened the building of the Revolutionary Party for Reunification in the face of great hardships and difficulties.

As a united Marxist-Leninist Party, a party of the working class, the Revolutionary Party for Reunification was born in the hard revolutionary fight of the south Korean revolutionaries and people against the U.S. imperialists and their stooges. With its emergence, broad masses of the oppressed and exploited people in south Korea have acquired a genuine defender of their class and national interests. The south Korean people today have a reliable political general staff in their revolutionary battle for freedom and liberation.

The political stand and the fighting goals of the Revolutionary Party for Reunification are explicitly stated in its Manifesto and Program, made public in the name of its Central Committee in Seoul in August of last year.

The Manifesto and the Program of the Revolutionary Party for Reunification emphasized that the guiding idea of the Party is the Marxist-Leninist idea of *Juche*. They declared that the ultimate objective of the Party is to build socialist and communist society, while its immediate objective is to carry out a people's democratic revolution against U.S. imperialism and fascist rule in south Korea, overthrowing the corrupt colonial and semi-feudal social system and setting up a people's democratic regime on its grave and, further, to fulfill the great cause of re-unification of our homeland, the nation's desire and aspiration.

The fighting goal and program put forth by the Revolutionary Party for Reunification reflect the law of socio-economic development and the unanimous aspirations of the people of all walks of life in south Korea. As such, they constitute the joint political program of all the patriotic, democratic forces in south Korea in their fight against the colonial rule of the U.S. imperialist aggressors and for the democratic development of society and the independent, peaceful reunification of our country. They constitute the aim of struggle of the entire south Korean people.

The organizations of the Revolutionary Party for Reunification took an active part in the June 3 Uprising of 1964 against the traitorous "ROK-Japan talks," the August Struggle of 1965 to reject the "ROK-Japan agreements," the struggle against the puppet presidential and puppet national assembly "elections" in 1967 and many other struggles, and are now playing a leading role in the revolutionary struggle of the south Korea people. In the course of struggle the Party has undergone steady revo-lutionary training and has gained the confidence of the south Korean people and increasing influence among them.

Today the south Korean revolutionaries are consolidating the organizations of the Revolutionary Party for Reunification, firmly rallying the patriotic people around it and are launching a heroic anti-U.S. struggle for national salvation: underground, in the mountains, in the prisons, and even on the gallows.

Comrades, in order to vanquish the counterrevolution and

achieve the victory of the revolution in south Korea, it is necessary to steadily strengthen the revolutionary forces. Only when the forces of the revolution are adequately prepared, can they react in time to repel the enemy's counterrevolutionary offensive and, further, meet the great revolutionary event in full readiness.

What is of paramount importance in preparing the revolutionary forces is to strengthen the Marxist-Leninist Party—the General Staff in the revolution—and rally the workers and peasants closely around it to build a firm central revolutionary force. The south Korean revolutionaries should strive to expand and strengthen Party forces everywhere there are workers, peasants and other revolutionary masses, and root themselves deeply in the masses. To expand and consolidate the mass base of the Party it is necessary to continue to set up mass organizations in various forms among the working people and to solidify them.

All the social groups interested in the revolution must be welded into a single political force at the same time that the main detachment of the revolution is being built up. Only in this way can the counterrevolutionary forces be isolated completely and the overwhelming supremacy of the revolutionary forces be guaranteed. The revolutionary organizations of south Korea should do everything possible to form an anti-U.S. united front for national salvation embracing all patriotic political parties, social organizations, different sectors of the people and individual public figures under the banner of anti-imperialism, anti-fascism and democratization. They should make particularly active efforts to firmly integrate the student youth into the revolutionary ranks and strengthen the organizational ties between them and the workers and peasants who constitute the main force of the revolution.

Only in the course of a widespread mass struggle can the revolutionary forces steadily grow in scope and strength. Only amid the flames of an active revolutionary struggle does the political awakening of the masses become intense; only then is the work of organizing them accelerated; and only then do the activists of the revolution become more numerous and the revolutionary organizations increase their militancy. The more urgent the task of increasing and developing the revolutionary forces in south Korea, the more actively should the mass struggle against the U.S. imperialist aggressors and their lackeys be organized and unfolded, and correct strategic and tactical guidance for it be ensured. What is important here is to analyze and judge the prevailing situation scientifically, taking due account of the requirements of the development of the revolution and the level of consciousness of the masses and, on this basis, put forth suitable fighting slogans and choose the right forms and methods of struggle, skillfully taking advantage of all possibilities, including the inner contradictions and weaknesses of the enemy. The south Korean revolutionaries and people should firmly push the revolutionary movement forward by correctly combining diverse forms and methods of struggle —political and economic struggles, legal, semi-legal and illegal struggles, violent and non-violent struggles, large- and small-scale struggles.

An important task facing the south Korean revolutionaries and patriotic people at the present stage is the positive development of the mass struggle for the democratization of society and against the colonial rule of U.S. imperialism and fascist suppression by its henchmen. It is important to organically link the political struggle against U.S. imperialist colonial rule and fascist military dictatorship and for the attainment of democratic rights—including freedoms of speech, the press, assembly, association and demonstration—with the economic struggle of the toiling masses for the right to exist. The struggle of the student youth for political liberty must be made more purposeful and conscious and their democratic movement must be closely combined with the political struggle of the workers and peasants. Revolutionary forces must be built up so as to crush counterrevolutionary violence by revolutionary violence, always answering violence with violence.

If the south Korean revolutionaries and people build a solid political army through struggle and constantly accumulate their revolutionary forces, they will be ready and able to meet the decisive hour of the revolution. In this way they will eventually topple the present reactionary regime and set up a people's democratic regime, thereby definitely achieving the objectives of the south Korean revolution.

True, the south Korean revolution still has a thorny path ahead, before it achieves victory. But neither the enemy's frenzied endeavors nor any number of trials and tribulations can check its triumphant advance and block the path of the south Korean revolutionaries and patriotic people who have risen in a sacred fight for freedom and liberation, deeply convinced of the justness of their cause.

The people in the southern half are not alone in their revolutionary struggle. They have a powerful revolutionary base in the northern half. Needless to say, the south Korean revolution is a struggle of the south Korean people themselves for their liberation from national and class oppression and exploitation by the U.S. imperialist aggressors and their minions. The oppressed and exploited masses can win freedom and emancipation only through their own revolutionary struggle. Therefore, the south Korean revolution must, in all situations, be made by the south Korean people on their own initiative. But it is the obligation and responsibility of the people in the northern half, as a part of the same nation, to actively support the south Korean people in their revolutionary struggle. The general international situation is now changing to the disadvantage of the counterrevolution and in favor of the revolution. The progressive peoples of all continents denounce U.S. imperialism for its aggressive policy on south Korea and strongly support and encourage the south Korean people in their righteous liberation struggle.

The disintegration of U.S. imperialist colonial rule and the triumph of the revolutionary cause of the people in south Korea are certain.

Comrades, the U.S. imperialist occupation of south Korea has partitioned our territory and split our nation; it has not only visited untold misery and suffering on the south Korean people but brought national calamity to the entire Korean people and set up a great obstacle to the coordinated development of Korean society as a whole.

To reunify the divided homeland is the greatest and most pressing national task for the entire Korean people at present. Its solution brooks not a moment's delay.

The whole world knows our Party's policy on national reunification. We have made it clear time and again that if democratic figures with a national conscience come to power in south Korea and demand the withdrawal of U.S. troops, release political prisoners and guarantee democratic freedoms, we are ready to hold negotiations with them any time and any place on the question of the peaceful reunification of the country. Even after the present south Korean rulers staged the fascist military coup and usurped power, we advanced the most fair and reasonable proposals for the reunification of our homeland and made consistent efforts to realize them. We did this in the hope that they would desist from their treacheries to the country and people and would take a truly national stand. More than once we proposed to the south Korean authorities that after the U.S. imperialist aggressor army had been driven out of south Korea, the north and the south should each reduce their armies to 100,000 men or less, conclude an agreement to refrain from using armed force against each other, initiate such measures as economic and cultural exchanges and visits of individuals between north and south and establish a unified, democratic government through a free north-south general election. We proposed that such a general election be held when the basic conditions are provided for reunifying the country peacefully in accordance with the free will of the Korean people; if such a general election were not immediately acceptable to them for some reason or other, a Confederation of north and south Korea would be established first as a transitional step for solving urgent matters of common concern for the nation and hastening the reunification of our homeland.

But the south Korean rulers have been dead set against the independent, peaceful reunification of the country, each time ignoring our just proposals which reflect the unanimous aspirations of the whole nation.

The south Korean puppets, under the aegis of the U.S. imperialists and the Japanese militarists, are yelling that the reunification of Korea must be a "reunification by prevailing over communism," and that it is necessary for them to foster their own power for this; they prattle about actions to "protect" south Korea against the fictitious "threat of southward aggression." This is nothing but a smokescreen covering their aggressive design to stifle the south Korean revolution, and invade the northern half of the Republic by force of arms. With such absurd pretexts, the enemy schemes to perpetuate the occupation of south Korea by the U.S. imperialist aggressor army on the one hand, and on the other, reinforces the aggressive armed forces on a large scale, expanding military installations and madly stepping up war preparations in south Korea.

The "reunification by prevailing over communism" vociferously advocated by the south Korean rulers means wiping out communism to attain "reunification." This is no more than a fantastic daydream, a feeble-minded babble. For 25 years now, the people in the northern half of the Republic, using communist ideas as their guiding principle, have been building an independent sovereign state, rich and strong, and creating their new, happy life. Communist ideas have taken firm root in the hearts of the people in the north and have been converted into a great indestructible material force. To reunify the country by excluding the Communists in Korea, is in fact, to reject reunification and leave south Korea forever in the hands of U.S. imperialism, as its colony.

As for the so-called "peaceful reunification program," much vaunted of late by the south Korean puppets, it is nothing but a strategic bit of political propaganda filled with lies and deceits from start to finish, devoid of any formula for the settlement of the question of national reunification. The "peaceful reunification program" and all other clamors of this type are aimed at dampening the ever-increasing trend in south Korea towards independent, peaceful reunification, disguising their treachery to the country and nation, confusing world public opinion, which supports our national reunification program.

How can we discuss the question of the reunification of the country with traitors to the nation who are blocking its independent, peaceful realization; using bayonets to repress the south Korean people's struggle for it; imploring the U.S. to continue its military occupation of south Korea; ushering into south Korea the aggressor forces of Japanese militarism; selling their fellow countrymen to foreign countries as slaves; and forcing young and middle-aged south Koreans into the war of aggression in Viet Nam as cannon fodder for the U.S. imperialists?

The peaceful reunification of our country is utterly unthinkable as long as the U.S. imperialist aggressor army and the present puppets remain in south Korea.

To achieve national reunification, it is essential to expel from south Korea the U.S. imperialist aggressors who are its main obstacle and liquidate their colonial rule, overthrow the present fascist military dictatorship and win the victory of the revolution. When a true people's regime is thus established in south Korea, the reunification of our homeland will be achieved easily by the united efforts of the socialist forces in the northern half of the Republic and the patriotic, democratic forces in south Korea.

No amount of frantic maneuvering by the U.S. imperialists and their minions can break the staunch fighting will of the Korean people to reunify the country. The entire people of north and south Korea will closely unite and vigorously fight the U.S. imperialists and their stooges to frustrate the insidious machinations of the enemy to perpetuate this national split. Thus, we will definitely achieve the reunification of our homeland.

The Revolutionary Peoples of Asia Will Win in Their Common Struggle Against U.S. Imperialism [Excerpt]

Speech at the Pyongyang Mass Meeting Welcoming Samdech Norodom Sihanouk, Head of State of Cambodia and Chairman of the National United Front of Kampuchea, August 6, 1971

Comrades and friends, for the final victory of the Korean revolution we should strengthen and develop our own internal revolutionary force in every way, while at the same time strengthening our solidarity with the international revolutionary forces.

Today the U.S. imperialists are still entrenched in south Korea, refusing to withdraw and are making desperate efforts to make Koreans fight Koreans. The Japanese militarists with the backing of the U.S. imperialists are stepping up their scheme to invade our country again. Under these circumstances we must not slacken vigilance even for a moment. We must continue to direct great efforts to strengthening our defense capacity, as well as stepping up socialist economic construction in order to make the defense of our fatherland impregnable in any emergency.

Holding aloft the banner of the *Juche* idea, under the wise leadership of our Party our people have followed the revolutionary line of independence, self-support and self-defense, and thereby successfully carried out the historic task of socialist industrialization and built up a defense potential strong enough to crush the imperialists any time they attack us.

Encouraged by the successes scored in the northern half of the Republic, the south Korean people are waging a staunch struggle to overthrow the military fascist dictatorship of the U.S. imperialists and their lackeys, shatter the Japanese militarists' scheme to invade our country again and attain freedom, liberation and the reunification of our fatherland. They are dealing heavy blows at the colonial rule of the U.S. imperialists.

Alarmed by a situation which is developing more and more in favor of the revolution as the days go by, the puppet clique of south Korea clings as always to the coattails of the U.S. imperialists and relies all the more on the Japanese militarists in a vain attempt to put off their doom. In an attempt to cover up their treacherous nature and stifle the movement for peaceful reunification, mounting with irresistible force among the south Korean people, they are noisily advertising their fraudulent "peaceful reunification programme." This stupid ruse, however, can fool no one, nor can it save the south Korean puppet clique from a doom already sealed.

The Government of the Democratic People's Republic of Korea has made consistent efforts to bring about the peaceful reunification of Korea. Again, last April it advanced an 8-point program for independent, peaceful reunification.

This time, too, the U.S. imperialists and the south Korean puppet clique have not replied to our fair and just program for peaceful reunification—a program reflecting the unanimous desire of the entire nation—and are only indulging in empty talk about peaceful reunification. If the south Korean rulers truly want peaceful reunification, to begin with they must not plead for the permanent stationing of U.S. troops but make them withdraw from south Korea. They must stop colluding with the Japanese militarists and stop bringing them into south Korea. They must stop suppressing the political parties, social organizations and democratic personages of south Korea who call for peaceful reunification but enable them to come out for north-south negotiations for the reunification of the country. They must proceed from the stand that the Korean question must be solved by the Koreans themselves.

Apart from the question as to whether or not the south Korean rulers accept our 8-point peaceful reunification program, if they truly want reunification, why are they afraid of contacts and negotiations between the north and the south?

We are ready to establish contact at any time with all political parties, including the Democratic Republican Party, and all social organizations and individual personages in south Korea.

If the south Korean rulers refuse even initial contacts between the north and the south and only give lip service to peaceful reunification, it will stir up more bitter hatred and wrath among the people. They are openly claiming that the question of reunification can only be discussed after 1973 when their "strength is built up" or even in the second half of the 1970's. Their motive is to bring the revived Japanese militarists into south Korea in full force by that time, and then realize their wild ambition of "reunification by prevailing over communism."

Our people will continue to struggle strenuously to step up socialist construction in the northern half of the Republic, to bring about the south Korean revolution by assisting the south Korean people and to get the question of reunification solved independently by the Korean people themselves on a democratic basis and in a peaceful way.

The Korean people's just struggle to force the U.S. imperialist aggressors to withdraw from south Korea, remove tension in Korea and attain the independent, peaceful reunification of our country, is bound to triumph with the constantly growing support and encouragement of the peace-loving people the world over.

New Year Address
[Excerpt]

January 1, 1972

Comrades, the aspirations of the entire people in north and south Korea for peaceful reunification are growing more than ever today. At Panmunjom representatives of the north and south Korean Red Cross organizations met for the first time in the 26 years after liberation to discuss the important question of alleviating the distress of our fellow countrymen living separated from each other in the north and the south. The entire people in north and south Korea are very glad that such contact between the north and the south has been materialized, though belatedly, and are unanimous in expressing the hope that the talks pave the sure way for pulling down the barriers between the north and the south and materializing the peaceful reunification of the country.

Precisely at this juncture the reactionaries and rulers in south Korea have proclaimed the so-called state of emergency, pleading the non-existent "threat of aggression from the north" as their excuse, and have gone into fascist tyranny against the south Korean people. Those bandits are fabricating all sorts of notorious fascist laws every day, suppressing all the elementary democratic liberties such as of speech, the press, assembly and association and keeping the south Korean society constantly in a state of unrest and fear. A few days ago they rigged up a monstrous fascist law entitled "special law on measures for national security" in the face of a strong objection from the opposition parties and the public. Such fascist acts of the south Korean reactionaries against the unanimous aspirations of the whole nation and the trend of the times are aimed primarily at suppressing the ever-growing tendency towards peaceful reunification among the south Korean people and frustrating contacts and negotiations between the north and the south.

Originally, the present puppet rulers in south Korea were the military gangsters who usurped the "power" by force of arms with the backing of the U.S. imperialists in order to hold back the trend towards peaceful reunification which was growing rapidly among the south Korean people following the April 19 Popular Uprising of 1960. After they assumed power as puppets, they put up such ostentatious slogans as "independence," "rehabilitation" and "modernization" in their attempt to deceive the south Korean people, but their true colors were exposed long ago in the eyes of the public. Over the past ten years south Korea has travelled not the way to "independence" but to complete dependence, not the way to "rehabilitation" and "modernization" but to total bankruptcy and ruin.

The south Korean puppet clique have lapsed into a serious political and economic crisis past recovery and this gives them an ever-growing unrest and despair. Though they are trying to find a way out of the blind alley by means of proclaiming the so-called state of emergency and starting a new fascist tyranny, this is no more than the death-bed struggle of the doomed.

The south Korean puppet clique are making noise about the fictitious "threat of aggression from the north" while declaring a "state of emergency," and this is an extremely underhand action to deceive the south Korean people and the world public, and beg their masters for a few more weapons and a few more dollars. The trend of history will never leave unchecked such a cowardly behavior of traitors to the nation. The fraudulent trick of those bandits will hoodwink nobody.

Recently the south Korean puppet clique have developed the

habit of clamoring that since we have completed war preparations, we will start invasion soon. True, we are building up our defense power. But it is by no means that we aim to solve the question of national reunification by force of arms. It is to defend the country and nation and safeguard our socialist gains from the aggression of the U.S. imperialists and the Japanese militarists.

Our armed forces are entirely for self-defense.

The power of the proletarian dictatorship will resist by employing force only when the imperialists, reactionary classes and counterrevolutionary elements use force against the revolution. This is the universal principle of Marxism-Leninism and a guide to action for the Government of our Republic. Therefore, it is nothing but absurd, false propaganda when the south Korean puppet clique clamor about the "threat of aggression from the north."

As facts show, no one is fooled now by the mendacious propaganda of the south Korean puppet clique. Rather, their fraudulent propaganda and fascist suppression arouse great indignation and protest among the south Korean people and world people. Even some of the reactionary ruling circles and reptile press in the United States and Japan say that the proclamation of the "state of emergency" in south Korea has not been caused by the threat of southward intrusion but is an invented political trick due to the internal situation, and is an attempt to tide over the social crisis. A Western press reported that the declaration of the "state of emergency" by the south Korean rulers is not due to the "threat of aggression from the north" but to many problems to be solved internally, and that it aims to smother the ever-growing discontent of the south Korean people caused by the acute economic crisis, and supress the demonstration struggle of the youth and students, the protest of the intellectuals and the resistance of the opposition parties.

The south Korean puppet clique should no longer entertain the foolish hope that the U.S. imperialists and Japanese militarists can deliver them from ruin. The times and circumstances have changed. The days are gone when the U.S. imperialists decided the internal affairs of other countries at their discretion; they have long been on the decline where they cannot escape their doom. The U.S. imperialists are now in a serious political and economic crisis at home and stand in total international isolation. The Sato clique of Japan is also staggering because of the discord within the ruling circles and the strong anti-government struggle of the broad sectors of the popular masses. In the last analysis, there is little difference between the positions of the south Korean puppet clique and those of their masters. Just as they were unable to relieve from ruin the Chiang Kai-shek gang of Taiwan and Thieu band of South Viet Nam, the U.S. imperialists and the Sato clique of Japan will never be able to save the south Korean puppet clique.

Even now when the situation is taking such a turn, the south Korean puppet clique keep clinging to the U.S. imperialists and the Japanese militarists in their efforts to maintain their puppet rule. They are begging U.S. imperialism not to "reduce" its aggressive armed forces in south Korea; the latter, finding itself in a scrape, is paying lip service to "cutback." The Japanese militarist aggressive forces have been called into south Korea again, this time by the puppet clique there. Such traitorous acts of the south Korean puppet clique against the nation only help to hasten their own ruin.

Furthermore, the south Korean puppet clique are dreaming of "reunification by prevailing over communism," with the backing of the U.S. imperialists and the Japanese militarists. This is really ridiculous nonsense.

History has already furnished an ample proof that nothing can destroy communism. The communist movement has over 100 years of history, counting only from the Paris Commune. All the imperialists and their lackeys have opposed communism, but so far none of them have succeeded in destroying it.

The successive puppet rulers of south Korea, too, without exception, have made every desperate attempt to oppose communism under the slogan of anti-communism. But communism, far from being destroyed in our country, has rather gained in scope and strength with each passing day. In the northern half of the Republic communist ideology became an absolutely dominant ideology long ago, and has turned into a great material force in all fields of politics, economy, culture and military. Communist ideology has struck deep roots even in the hearts of many south Korean revolutionaries and people. Such being the situation now, it is quite clear that the south Korean puppet clique's dream of "reunification by prevailing over communism" is under no circumstances likely to come true.

The south Korean puppet clique must face the stern reality of today. If they do not renounce the outdated way of thinking that they are following now, but persist in the dirty act of betraying the country and the nation, going against the historical trend, they will not be able to find a way out. If the south Korean rulers want to find some way out, they should not resort to sordid trickery, as they are doing now, but should honestly admit their crimes, stop their acts of selling out the country and the nation to the U.S. imperialists and Japanese militarists, discontinue their fascist suppression of the south Korean people at once, and respond to the earnest call of the Government of our Republic to realize peaceful reunification through negotiations between the Koreans themselves.

The Government of the Democratic People's Republic of Korea has advanced time and again the most fair and reasonable proposals for the independent, peaceful reunification of the country. Last year alone, the Government of the Republic put forward 8-point proposals for peaceful reunification at the Fifth Session of the Fourth Supreme People's Assembly; particularly in our speech on August 6, we once again clarified our readiness to make contact at any time with all political parties, including the Democratic Republican Party, social organizations and individual personalities in south Korea. All our proposals and suggestions for the independent, peaceful reunification of the country have met with enthusiastic support and response from the broad sectors of the people and personalities from various strata in south Korea, to say nothing of the people in the northern half of the Republic. The south Korean rulers, too, must have the courage to respond to our fair and just proposals, keeping abreast of this nation-wide trend. This will be the only correct act befitting them as Koreans. And only when they do this, I supose, will the south Korean puppet rulers be able to redeem themselves even in some measure from the crimes they have committed against the country and the people, though a little too late, and find a way out to save themselves.

If the south Korean rulers renounce their reliance on the outside forces and depart from the road of treachery to the nation and return to the position which is truly Korean, we will not ask about their past but will peacefully settle the question of national reunification with them.

In the future too, our Party and the Government of the Republic will continue to advocate the independent, peaceful reunification of the country and make every effort for its materialization. But if the south Korean puppet clique do not respond to us in spite of our patient efforts, but keep following the road of betraying the nation, they will ruin themselves, without redeeming their crimes, as traitors forever.

U.S. imperialism is on the decline today, but its aggressive nature remains unchanged and it continues its death-bed struggle. The signboard of "peace" put up by the U.S. imperialists is nothing but a screen to mislead people. Nixon is a rascal, more vicious and crafty than anyone else. The U.S. imperialists do not give up their wild ambition to perpetuate our country's split and make south Korea their permanent colony. They instigate the south Korean puppet clique to continue with aggressive provocations against the northern half of the Republic. And the Japanese militarists, revived by U.S. imperialism, openly reveal their wild design to invade our country again. The Japanese militarists, the "shock force" of U.S. imperialism, are fully prepared to take part in an aggressive war against our country and are watching for a chance of aggression all the time.

Under these conditions all the people in north and south Korea should sharpen their vigilance against the aggressive maneuvering of the U.S. imperialists and Japanese militarists. Our people can never allow the U.S. imperialists and Japanese militarists to rob them of their country and become slaves for the latter, and repeat the disgraceful history of 1910 when their country was lost. The entire Korean people, irrespective of different political views and religious beliefs, should unite firmly under the banner of the country's defense and independent reunification, and wage an active struggle to frustrate the maneuvers of the U.S. imperialists and Japanese militarists for aggression.

Even those who committed crimes against the country and the nation in the past should turn out valiantly in a nationwide struggle against the aggression of the U.S. imperialists and Japanese militarists and for the independent reunification of the country, thereby making up for their crimes. If they want to atone for their crimes against the nation, the south Korean rulers should also join in this struggle. They should struggle to drive out the U.S. imperialists, instead of imploring them not to pull out of south Korea, and should not try to usher in the Japanese militarists into south Korea but should fight to smash their maneuvers for resumption of aggression.

If all the people in the north and the south wage a struggle in firm, monolithic unity, they will be fully able to frustrate the invasion of any imperialists. If the U.S. imperialists and Japanese militarists dare to unleash a war of aggression in our country, the entire north and south Korean people will unite and fight a showdown battle against the enemies, annihilate the aggressors completely and reunify the divided country.

This year the General Association of Korean Residents in Japan (*Chongryon*) organizations and all the Korean nationals in Japan should continue a vigorous struggle to actively protect all the policies of the Workers' Party of Korea and the Government of the Republic, defend their democratic national rights and further advance national education. The Korean nationals in Japan should fight unyieldingly to expedite the peaceful reunification of the homeland. In firm unity with the Japanese people and broad democratic forces of Japan, they should unfold a dynamic struggle against the Japanese militarists' maneuvers to reinvade south Korea and the hostile policy of the Japanese reactionaries toward the Democratic People's Republic of Korea. In particular, the Korean nationals in Japan should smash up the splitting acts and all the subversive activities of the U.S. and Japanese reactionaries and the factionalists, further consolidate their ranks, rally themselves closely around the *Chongryon* and wage a vigorous struggle.

The international situation is now developing in favor of the

revolutionary cause of our people. The anti-imperialist, revolutionary forces of the world are growing in scope and strength with
each passing day; more and more countries actively support
and encourage our people in their struggle for independent,
peaceful reunification.

Our Party and the Government of the Republic will, this year
too, try hard to strengthen their militant solidarity with the
revolutionary peoples of the world and promote relations of
friendship and cooperation with the peoples of all the countries
supporting our people's righteous struggle. In particular, we will
unfold a powerful joint struggle against the U.S. and Japanese
imperialists and their stooges, in firm unity with the peoples in
China, Indo-China, Japan and other Asian countries. By so doing,
we will smash up the U.S. imperialists' notorious "Nixon
doctrine" and the Japanese militarists' machination for overseas
aggression, thus safeguarding peace in Asia and the rest of the
world and bringing about a more favorable turn in our people's
cause of independent, peaceful reunification.

On Immediate Political and Economic Policies of the Democratic People's Republic of Korea and Some International Problems [Excerpt]

Answers to the Questions Raised by Newsmen of the Japanese Newspaper "Yomiuri Shimbun", January 10, 1972

Today the general situation of our country is developing very favorably for the struggle of our people for the independent, peaceful reunification of the country.

The successes of socialist construction made in the northern half of the country under the banner of the *Juche* idea further consolidate the political and economic basis for the independent reunification of the country, give great hope and confidence to the people of the southern half and vigorously rouse them to the struggle for the peaceful reunification of the country.

Lately, a tendency towards peaceful reunification is rapidly growing and the struggle against the fascist rule and for the democratization of society is gaining momentum as never before in south Korea. The massive advance of the student youth and people that has continued before and after the "election" of the puppet president held last year, and brisk arguments about national reunification in the public and political circles show that the tendency of opposing the present ruling system and demanding peaceful reunification is rising in south Korea with an irresistible force.

As our policy for the peaceful reunificatiion enjoyed unanimous support not only of the Korean people but of the broad public opinion of the world, and the tendency towards peaceful reunification grew in south Korea, even the south Korean authorities who had rejected any contact between the north and the south could not but come out to the north-south Red Cross talks, pressed by the trend of the times. Though it is rather late and the scope of the problems being discussed is limited, the preliminary talks between the north and south Red Cross organizations now being held at Panmunjom are very significant, at any rate since Koreans have gotten together to discuss internal affairs of the nation. It can be said that this is a step forward in the struggle of our people for reunifying the divided country peacefully.

Our stand on the talks between the north and south Red Cross organizations is clear. We want to mitigate, even a day earlier, the sufferings our people are undergoing owing to the division, by bringing the talks to a success with all our sincerity and pave the way, with it as a stepping stone, to the peaceful reunification of the country.

But the stand of the south Korean authorities is quite opposite. From the first day they were compelled to come out to the talks, they dragged on the talks under this or that pretext and poured cold water upon the growing tendency towards the peaceful reunification, saying: "Don't get too much excited," and "It is premature." Moreover, saying that we would soon "invade the south" because we have already finished war preparations, they proclaimed a "state of national emergency" and are newly trumping up various evil fascist laws to buttress it, and deliberately aggravating the situation.

Such a racket kicked up by the south Korean puppet clique cannot be interpreted otherwise than a design to prolong their remaining days by putting down the ever-growing tendency towards peaceful reunification in south Korea, frustrating contacts and negotiations between the north and the south and perpetuating the split of the country. It is not an accident that even some reactionary ruling circles and government-controlled press in the United States and Japan say that the proclamation of the "state of emergency" in south Korea is not because of the threat of "southward aggression" but, rather, a political trick hatched up because of the internal situation.

With such a foolish trick the south Korean rulers can deceive nobody and solve nothing.

It seems, that frightened by the rapid change of the internal and external situations to their disadvantage, they are going on the rampage. But, they need to cool their heads and think over matters calmly.

Now the times and situation have changed.

The situation today is different from that of the 40's when the U.S. imperialists could divide our country into north and south, abusing the name of the "UN." The day has gone when the U.S. imperialists could meddle in the affairs of other countries and rule the roost.

Now the U.S. imperialists and the Japanese militarists can hardly attend to their own affairs.

We think the time has come when the south Korean rulers should give up the anti-national stand they have held to seek a way out by clinging to the coattails of the U.S. imperialist aggressors and ushering in the Japanese aggressors, turning their back on the compatriots.

If the south Korean rulers are to find a true way out, they should come to the national stand, give up even now their absurd assertion that they would "build up strength" with the backing of outside forces to overpower north Korea by force and attain "reunification by prevailing over communism," and accept our fair and aboveboard proposals to reunify the country in a peaceful way by joining the efforts of the Korean people themselves.

You asked me about our concrete program for the reunification of the country. Our program for national reunification is not different from the previous one. We have invariably maintained that the question of our country's reunification, an internal affair of our nation, should be solved not by the interference of outside forces but by the efforts of the Korean people themselves, not by means of war but in a peaceful way.

We reclarified the program for the independent, peaceful reunification of the country in the 8-point proposals for national salvation advanced at a session of the Supreme People's Assembly of the Democratic People's Republic of Korea held in April last year, in the speech made on August 6 last year and in the New Year Address this year. We will invariably make all our efforts in the future to realize the program.

A successful conclusion of the talks now going on between the north and south Red Cross organizations amid the great interest of the whole nation will create a favorable atmosphere for the peaceful reunification of the country.

The south Korean authorities, talking about some sort of "stage," prattle that this can be done and that cannot be done and that only some kind of undertakings must be done first and the other things be deferred. This is a delaying tactic and is not an attitude for solving problems.

If the north-south Red Cross talks yield good results and mutual and free traffic is realized between the families, relatives and friends torn apart in the north and the south, their sufferings will be lessened and, at the same time, the frozen sentiment between north and south will be thawed and mutual understanding deepened in this course.

It is a matter of vital importance for the peaceful reunification of the country, as well as for peace in Asia and the rest of the world, to remove tension in our country.

In order to remove tension in Korea, it is necessary, first of all, to replace the Korean Armistice Agreement with a peace agreement between north and south. We hold that a peace agreement should be concluded between north and south and the armed forces of north and south Korea be cut drastically under the conditions where the U.S. imperialist aggressor troops are withdrawn from south Korea.

We have made it clear more than once that we have no intention to "invade the south." If the south Korean rulers have no intention to "march north for reunification," there will be no reason for them to refuse to conclude a peace agreement between north and south. If they truly want peace in our country and peaceful reunification, they should agree to conclude a peace agreement between north and south, instead of clamoring about the fictitious "threat of southward aggression."

We advocate strengthening contacts and ties between north and south and holding north-south political negotiations to solve the question of national reunification.

Many problems arise in putting an end to the tragedy of national split and reunifying the country peacefully. All these problems can be satisfactorily solved only through political negotiations between north and south.

We are ready to have negotiations with all political parties of south Korea including the Democratic Republican Party, the New Democratic Party and the Nationalist Party at any time and at any place agreed upon. Now the south Korean authorities are talking this or that without having a meeting. It is not an attitude for solving the question of reunification peacefully to reject negotiations, talking about "peaceful reunification" only in words. In order to solve the question of the reunification of the country peacefully, various political parties of north and south Korea are required to hold bilateral or multilateral negotiations briskly for exchanging political views on national reunification and finding a reasonable way for peaceful reunification.

We always keep our door open to anyone for negotiations and contacts between the north and the south. If anyone, though he committed crimes against the country and the people, sincerely repents his past doings and takes a road of patriotism for the peaceful reunification of the country, we will not ask about his crimes but gladly negotiate with him about the question of the country's reunification.

When all the Koreans unite and fight along the road for the reunification of the country, we will surely be able to drive out the U.S. and Japanese aggressors, tide over the crisis of national ruin created in south Korea, and achieve the peaceful reunification of the country without fail. We are sure that though the question of Korean reunification is still complicated there is a prospect of peacefully solving it sooner or later in accordance with the will of our people and on the principle of national self-determination.

Talk with Journalists of the U.S. Newspaper, New York Times

May 26, 1972

I am sure you have seen for yourselves and sensed how the Korean people feel toward the United States here in our country.

They do not have good sentiments toward the United States. Our people have a very strong anti-U.S. feeling. Probably this feeling has offended you Americans.

It is natural that the Korean people should have ill feeling toward the United States. U.S. imperialism is the agressor which has invaded our country. No people can have warm feelings toward an aggressor who invades their country, can they?

The Korean people's anti-U.S. sentiments grew very strong, particularly because they suffered too much damage at the hands of the U.S. imperialists during the Fatherland Liberation War.

During this war, they suffered tremendous damage because of the U.S. imperialists' barbarous acts of aggression. I do not think there is any Korean who did not sustain a loss in the war. Every Korean suffered a loss in some way or other. If he did not suffer personally, at least his family, relatives, or friends did.

In Pyongyang, for example, the indiscriminate bombing of the U.S. imperialists left few houses intact. The entire city was reduced to ashes and tens of thousands of people were killed in cold blood. The same was true in Wonsan, Hamhung and other cities. Even our villages were all burned to ashes in the last days of the war.

Having suffered such severe damage at the hands of the U.S. imperialists, the Korean people cannot have good sentiments toward the United States.

Even after the armistice the United States continued an unfriendly attitude toward our country.

The Armistice Agreement stipulated that a political conference of the two sides would be held immediately after the war to settle the Korean question by peaceful means. However, the United States did not abide by this stipulation. As a result, our country is still in a state of ceasefire today. No peace agreeement has been concluded and there has been no progress in the work of solving the Korean question peacefully. Therefore, I always tell our people that generations are changing, but the target of our struggle remains the same.

The U.S. authorities have persisted in their aggressive acts against our country in violation of the Armistice Agreement. Even after the *Pueblo* incident, the United States continued its aerial reconnaissance of our country. This places our country in a perpetual de facto state of war.

As this state of war has continued since the ceasefire, we have been forced to step up building our defense and invest heavily in it. Frankly speaking, this enormous expenditure on defense building has, to a certain extent, slowed down the rise in the living standards of the people. Our people also blame the United States for this.

Thus, they have strong anti-U.S. feelings because they suffered great damage at the hands of the U.S. imperialists during the Fatherland Liberation War. Moreover, they have ill feeling toward the United States because the U.S. imperialists have been unfriendly toward our country and continued aggressive acts in violation of the Armistice Agreement even in the postwar period.

The tense situation forces us to continue to step up preparations against war. We make no secret of this. Who can guarantee that the U.S. imperialists will not attack our country again? Neither you nor I, nor anyone else. So we are openly making war preparations in order to defend the country from enemy aggression.

The most important thing in our war preparations is to teach all our people to hate U.S. imperialism. Otherwise, we will not be able to defeat the U.S. imperialists who boast of their technological superiority.

Therefore, we are intensifying ideological education, to imbue the people with hatred for U.S. imperialism. I think this is quite a natural and correct thing for us to do. We do not have to stop the anti-U.S. education we have been giving to our people or conceal the fact that we are educating them in anti-U.S. ideas just because you come to our country, do we?

You must understand our people's ill feeling toward the United States.

You have just said that you hope this abnormal situation between our country and the United States will improve. So do we. We do not want to have many enemies.

Now, let me answer the questions you have raised.

To begin with, I would like to refer to the question of relations between the Democratic People's Republic of Korea and the United States.

You ask me what positive measures should be taken to end the abnormal state of affairs between Korea and the United States. In our opinion this is a very simple matter.

The relations between our country and the United States depend entirely on the attitude of the U.S. government. If the U.S. government changes its policy towards us, we will do the same toward the United States.

If the U.S. government wants to improve its relations with our country, it must, first of all, stop interfering in our internal affairs so that the Koreans can settle the question of Korean reunification independently. It is nearly 20 years now since the Armistice Agreement was signed, so why should U.S. troops continue to occupy south Korea under the guise of "United Nations forces"? Some people say that the U.S. troops are staying on in south Korea to protect it because we might "invade the

south." This is a lie. We have declared time and again that we
have no intention of invading the south. It is high time to put an
end to the situation where U.S. troops play policemen in south
Korea under the emblem of "United Nations forces."

The U.S. government disquiets us not only because it has
stationed its armed force in south Korea but because it is helping
to revive Japanese militarism. We are not happy about the U.S.
assistance in the revival of Japanese militarism. We can see from
the joint communique of Nixon and Sato of 1969 that the United
States is bringing Japanese militarism into south Korea as its
agent for aggression against Korea and instigating it to interfere
in our country's internal affairs. Following the announcement of
the communique, Sato openly declared that he would interfere
in Korea's internal affairs. This is another aspect of the unfriendly attitude of the U.S. government toward our country.

On the Korean question in the United Nations, the U.S. government is also taking an unwarranted attitude toward our
country. It advocates inviting south Korea to the United Nations
unconditionally while attaching conditions to inviting us. It al-
leges that we do not respect the United Nations Charter, though
we have never violated or ignored it. The United States insists
that it will allow us to attend the UN General Assembly only if
we recognize the unlawful resolutions on the Korean question
which were adopted in the United Nations. How can we go to
the UN General Assembly under this condition? Furthermore,
the United States has been instigating the "United Nations
Commission for the Unification and Rehabilitation of Korea" to
give annual reports full of lies and fabrications about our country, thus continuing hostile propaganda against us.

Because the U.S. government has invariably pursued such an
unfriendly policy toward our country, there has been no improvement in Korea-U.S.relations and the reunification of our
country has been greatly hampered.

If the United States wants to improve its relations with our
country, it must stop interfering in our internal affairs so that
the Koreans can reunify their country by themselves, withdraw
its troops disguised as "UN forces" and dissolve the "United

Nations Commission for the Unification and Rehabilitation of Korea." It must not further the partition of the Korean nation but support its reunion. As long as the United States keeps our country divided, our attitude toward the United States will not change. The Korean peninsula is now cut into two parts. If the U.S. troops pull out of south Korea and foreign interference stops, the Koreans will be able to find a common denominator which will enable them to reunify their country by themselves. Furthermore, if the U.S. troops get out of south Korea, I think the Koreans will come to terms easily and our people's anti-U.S. feeling will gradually lessen.

When U.S. President Nixon looked at the Great Wall during his visit to China he said that the barriers dividing nations should be pulled down. If the U.S. government wants to put these words into practice, it must begin with Korea. These days Nixon says he is going to improve relations with China as well as with the Soviet Union. Why, then, should the United States keep its military bases in south Korea? The United States has argued that it keeps them there to prevent communist expansion. Now that it is going to have good relations with the big socialist countries, we consider that there is no excuse for keeping military bases in south Korea. So the United States must quit south Korea at once, dismantling all its military bases and withdrawing its aggressor army.

If the United States wants to better its relations with our country, it must also stop helping to revive Japanese militarism and stop bringing it into south Korea. The United States is trying to substitute Japanese militarism for itself in its invasion of south Korea and reduce south Korea to a commodity market and appendage of Japan. This is an unfriendly, hostile act against our people. The U.S. government must discontinue such unfriendly acts against our country.

If the U.S. government gives up its unfriendly act against our country and stops obstructing our reunification, then there will be no reason why we should be antagonistic to the United States. So we say that the relations between the Democratic People's Republic of Korea and the United States depend not on us, but entirely on the attitude of the U.S. government. We will closely watch the policy the United States adopts toward our country in the future.

The U.S. government should improve relations not only with big countries, but with small countries as well. We do not think improved U.S. relations with big countries will greatly influence its relations with small countries. In fact, the U.S. government has not yet changed its attitude in its relations with small countries.

In the joint communique of the People's Republic of China and the United States, the latter declared that it supports the relaxation of tension on the Korean peninsula and contact between north and south Korea. As for what influence the United States will exert on south Korea in this respect, we must wait and see. If the United States does not support the relaxation of tension in Korea and north-south contact in the future, it will mean that it uttered empty words under pressure.

Our people remember what Nixon said in China. What interests me most is that he said that no barriers should divide the people of the world. We are watching how he is going to put his words into practice.

You asked me if moves such as an exchange of journalists and cultural interchange to promote mutual understanding and reduce tension were possible between the two countries even before the U.S. troops are withdrawn from south Korea. I will answer this briefly.

Frankly, we cannot understand what interests Americans to come to our country. We do not think our people would bring back anything interesting if they visited the United States in the present situation.

We do not mean that we want to shut the door to relations with the United States. But we consider that as long as the fundamental problem between the two countries remains unsolved, an exchange of journalists or cultural interchange would be of little significance.

I am told you feel uncomfortable in our country. If other Americans come here they will return with the same uncomfortable feeling.

We are now intensifying anti-U.S. education among our younger generation so that they will not forget their enemy. As long as the U.S. government's hostile policy toward our country remains unchanged, our policy toward the United States will not change either. Therefore, Americans will not get good impressions here until the fundamental problem between the two countries is solved. If many Americans come to our country in the future, and go back with uncomfortable feelings, we think such visits will not be beneficial.

If the U.S. government discards its hostile policy toward our country, our anti-U.S. feelings may be lessened. Only then will visits and interchange between the two countries be fruitful and interesting to both sides.

Since the U.S. government does not alter its hostile policy toward our country, mutual visits had better be limited in scope, as at present. We do not think that there is no need at all for our journalists to visit the United States. In our opinion, it is necessary for them to go there in order to let the American people hear our true voice, because at present you only hear the voice of the south Korean rulers. We welcome visits by American journalists and democratic figures on a limited scale. Such visits and interchange will help promote understanding between the two peoples.

In the light of our experience in receiving you now, I think it would be a good idea for us to explain to future American visitors how we are conducting anti-U.S. education among our people before they start going on visits.

Next I want to refer to a few points concerning Korea's reunification.

You asked me whether it would be possible to deal with the Korean question in the same way as the Viet Nam question was dealt with at the Geneva Conference in 1954. We think we need not deal with the Korean question in such a way.

The Korean question must be solved by the Koreans themselves on the principle of national self-determination without any foreign interference. Only then can the reunification of our country be achieved peacefully.

The Soviet Union and China actively support this program for national reunification. The Soviet and Chinese governments have issued statements on many occasions supporting our country's program for peaceful reunification.

A prerequisite for the independent settlement of the question of Korean reunification without foreign interference is that the U.S. troops must be withdrawn from south Korea. No war will break out in Korea after they are withdrawn.

When the U.S. troops pull out of south Korea and the people of north and south Korea are united, we can reunify Korea quickly and frustrate the Japanese militarists' maneuvers to invade Korea again. The Korean people can achieve national unity by their own efforts.

As you know, we are now having contacts with south Korea through the preliminary talks between the north and south Korean Red Cross organizations. Of course, as for the prospects and the results of the talks, we will have to wait and see. But we think that if we Koreans sit down at a conference table, we can find ways for removing the distrust and misunderstanding between the north and the south and attaining national unity.

The north and south Koreans are cold to each other, and distrust and misunderstand each other in many respects because they have had no opportunity to sit down together in one place.

We think distrust and misunderstanding exist between the north and south Koreans on a number of questions.

We believe that the south Korean rulers may invade the northern half of the Republic with the support of the United States and the Japanese militarist forces. The south Korean rulers labor under the misunderstanding that we might attack south Korea. They are also raising "anti-communist" clamors, asserting that we are trying to "communize" south Korea. Due to such distrust and misunderstanding, no progress has yet been made on the question of Korean reunification.

We believe that if we Koreans sit down together, we will be able to remove distrust and misunderstanding and find common denominators and, on this basis, achieve national unity.

These days the south Korean rulers are clamoring for the independent reunification of the country, advocating, though in words only, "self-help," "self-reliance," "self-defense." If we interpret this favorably, we can see some similarity with the idea of independence, self-reliance and self-defense which we advocate.

If we find and develop these common denominators one by one, it will be possible to reach an agreement on achieving national unity.

The difference in social systems in the north and the south must not be made an obstacle to the promotion of national unity and the attainment of reunification.

At present, some foreign journalists say there are two opposite poles in Korea—north Korea's communist system and south Korea's capitalist system—and these two poles cannot be integrated. Once these two poles touch, they say, war will break out again in Korea.

We do not regard south Korea as a capitalist society in the true sense of the word. There are no big monopoly capitalists in south Korea, only a few comprador capitalists. Of course, we are against comprador capitalists. We oppose them because they obstruct the development of the national economy. But we are not against national capitalists and small and medium entrepreneurs. We can say that south Korean society is no more than a society which is just starting to take the road of capitalism, or is inclined to capitalism, or is being influenced by capitalism, or believes in capitalism, or something like that. This does not mean that there is no difference in the social systems in the north and the south.

It is true that there are now differences in ideas and beliefs between the north and the south. But we think we must transcend these differences for the sake of national unity. We have no intention of imposing our socialist system on south Korea. Unless its present rulers try to force us to replace our socialist system with another, there is no reason why we cannot achieve national unity.

If the north and the south establish the principle of each not imposing its social system on the other, then there is no need to fight each other with arms. If neither side is forced to give up its political beliefs, is there any reason for the people of one and the same nation to fight?

It is possible that a country may have different political systems and that people with different beliefs may live together in one country. What political system should be established in south Korea is a matter for the south Korean people themselves to decide. So we consider that even after the country is reunified the present social systems in the north and the south may continue as they are, and the people who have different beliefs may live together in Korea. What is needed here is mutual trust and respect.

We always maintain that our homeland should be reunified independently and peacefully without foreign interference. Furthermore, we hold that the unity of the entire nation should be achieved under conditions in which both sides trust and respect each other, despite the different social systems in the north and the south.

In a speech on August 6 last year, we pointed out that we were ready to have contacts even with the Democratic Republican Party, the ruling party of south Korea. This stems from our desire to create mutual respect.

If the north and the south join hands and make tireless efforts, we will be able to eliminate mutual misunderstanding and distrust, and achieve the reunification of the country independently on a democratic basis. Our country cannot be reunified if outside forces meddle in the Korean question. Foreigners cannot rid our nation of distrust and misunderstanding. That is why we oppose interference of any outside force in the Korean question.

We believe that if there is no outside interference in the Korean question and foreign countries give up obstructionist machinations, the reunification of Korea will definitely be attained the way we are advocating, though it may take time.

You said you want to know what practical measures we are taking to bring about the independent, peaceful reunification of the country. I will outline them briefly.

We are calling for mail exchange and mutual visits and trade and economic cooperation as well between the north and the south.

As for mutual visits of personages we think it also desirable for our deputies to the Supreme People's Assembly and the "national assemblymen" of south Korea to visit each other. If "national assemblymen" of south Korea come to the northern half of the Republic and our deputies to the Supreme People's Assembly go to south Korea and if they sit down at one table and exchange views openheartedly through such mutual visits, it will be a good thing for the reunification of our homeland. It is by no means a bad thing. We want contacts not only with south Korean "national assemblymen" but also with a broad spectrum of political and public figures in south Korea. In other words, we hold that all the political parties and social organizations of north and south Korea should get together in a political consultative conference and exchange wide-ranging views on the question of national reunification.

Furthermore, we have proposed that, if it is impossible to reunify the country at once, a confederation be set up. This means forming a supreme national council with representatives of the north and south Korean governments, mainly for consulting and coordinating on matters concerning the national interests of Korea, while maintaining the present different political systems in north and south Korea as they are for the time being.

We have also more than once proposed economic intercourse between the north and the south, proceeding from the immediate interests of the nation. If economic cooperation materializes and we give south Korea what we have in sufficiency and receive what it has in plenty, the economy of both parts will develop more rapidly.

We have proposed cultural and scientific exchanges between the north and the south.

In addition, we maintain that a peace agreement should be concluded between the north and the south, stipulating that each side refrains from the use of arms against the other and that the numerical strength of the armed forces of the two sides be reduced after the withdrawal of all foreign troops from south

112   KIM IL SUNG

Korea. The present arms race between the north and the south
is having a considerable effect on the living standards of the
people.

We are doing all we can to remove the tension and bring
about contact and exchange between the north and the south.
True, if mutual visits are made, capitalist influence may be
brought into the northern half of the Republic. But we are not in
the least afraid of this. We keep our door open so that south
Koreans can visit the northern half of the Republic at any time. It
is not we but the south Korean rulers who are keeping the door
closed. Everything will be settled easily once the south Korean
authorities open their door.

But the south Korean rulers are very much afraid to do this.
Having declared a "state of emergency" under the pretext of a
fictitious "threat of aggression from the north," they are playing
all sorts of tricks while the preliminary talks are going on between
the north and south Korean Red Cross organizations. They are
ruthlessly suppressing those south Koreans who desire reunification. They are even prohibiting "national assemblymen"
of the Democratic Republican Party from talking with their
New Democratic Party colleagues in the puppet national
assembly. The south Korean rulers are now raising an "anti-
communist" clamor, holding "anti-communist rallies" and
"meetings for the annihilation of communism and against
espionage activities" in all parts of south Korea.

We have no intention of invading south Korea, nor do we
want to impose our socialist system on south Korea. Nevertheless, the south Korean rulers have declared a "state of
emergency" under the pretext of a "threat of aggression from
the north" and are intensifying their fascist repression of the
south Korean people and clamoring for "reunification through
the annihilation of communism." This is not an attitude helpful
to national reunification. Their hullabaloo is designed not to
bring about a close relationship between the north and the south
but to estrange them further. It is intended to prevent the country
from being reunified. By "reunification through the annihilation
of communism," the south Korean rulers mean to achieve
reunification after wiping out the Communists in Korea. In the

final analysis, this means that they oppose reunification and want to perpetuate the partition. We do not know who is the author of this racket in south Korea. But we think it betrays their weakness.

We will continue our patient efforts to bring about contacts and dialogue between the north and the south.

We are at present gravely concerned about south Korea's economic subjection to Japan. If the south Korean rulers keep the door between the north and the south closed, Japanese capital will penetrate south Korea, and the latter will become completely subjected to Japan economically.

We do not forget the history of the Japanese imperialists' invasion of our country. They began worming their way into Korea in 1894 under the pretext of protecting Japanese residents in Korea. From then on our country began falling into the status of a Japanese colony.

Japanese militarism revived under the wing of U.S. imperialism is now scheming to invade Korea again. We read an article in the Japanese magazine *World Weekly* which quoted Japanese militarist leaders as saying that Korea should not be reunified for at least a quarter of a century. This shows that the Japanese militarists are watching for a chance to invade Korea again.

We have to heighten our vigilance against the Japanese militarists. We are fully informing all our people, and especially the younger generation, on the history of Japanese militarist aggression in our country so that they will not forget it but keep sharp vigilance against Japanese militarism.

Our country has not yet been reunified, but remains divided into north and south because of the reactionary maneuvers of the south Korean rulers and the obstructionist activities of outside forces.

Therefore, we think that all the north and south Korean people must unite firmly and struggle actively against the outside forces that hamper the reunification of our country.

You asked me about the relations between our country and Japan. I will touch on this briefly now.

The improvement of relations between our country and Japan

depends on the attitude the Japanese government takes.

Good-neighbor relations have not been established up to this date solely because the Japanese government has followed a hostile policy toward our country. The successive cabinets of the Japanese government, from Yoshida to Sato, including those of Kishi and Ikeda, have adopted an unfriendly attitude and a hostile policy toward our country.

If the Japanese government gives up its hostile policy toward our country and wants to establish friendly relations with us, we are fully ready to respond.

However, as long as the Japanese government pursues a hostile policy and takes an unfriendly attitude toward our country, we do not want to improve relations between the two countries by resorting to sycophant diplomacy. The smaller a country is, the greater self-respect its people must have. If the peoples of small countries do not even have self-respect, they cannot survive. We do not want to go to Heaven by turning our right cheek after we have been hit on the left. We have no thought of throwing our self-respect away.

You asked me what is the best gift I could give to our people. It is the reunification of the country.

The Korean people are one people of the same blood. But they are divided because their country is not yet reunified. This is our greatest grief.

At present, because of an artificial barrier in our country many people live separated from their families and relatives for a long time, unable to meet each other, write letters or hear about each other's fate, alive or dead. The artificial barrier which causes this tragic state of affairs must be pulled down as soon as possible and our homeland reunified without fail.

Once our country is reunified, our people will lead as good a life as others, and will live peacefully with the different peoples of the world according to the principles of equality and mutual respect.

From ancient times, the Korean people have been industrious and resourceful. Our people went through suffering and were long subjected to national humiliation, oppression and exploitation, and to aggression by foreign invaders. So, if our people in north and south Korea join efforts and strive to build a new society, we will be able to live as well as others and our country will become a rich, powerful, independent and sovereign state.

Our country has a fairly large population and abundant natural resources. We have trained a large number of competent cadres of our own. Immediately after liberation we had few able technicians. The Japanese imperialists would not pass technology on to the Koreans and even prevented them from learning it. They were so adamant about preventing Koreans from acquiring technical knowledge that before liberation there were only four Korean locomotive drivers. They allowed only Japanese to be locomotive drivers and at best, let Koreans be stokers. In order not to repeat this bitter experience, we devoted great efforts after liberation to training our own cadres. As a result, we have half a million technicians and specialists today. On the basis of the successes already achieved in training cadres, we are planning to increase their number to one million during the Six-Year Plan.

As you see, we have a big population, rich natural resources and a huge army of technicians. So when the country is re-unified, we can build a rich and strong country and guarantee our people affluence in a short time.

I will give a brief answer to your question on what was the most difficult of our struggles.

We have had so many difficult struggles that I cannot tell you about them all here and now.

To my mind, one of the most difficult was the struggle to rise up out of the debris after the war.

In the three-year war, every town and village was razed to the ground and every industrial enterprise reduced to ashes. When the war ended, we had to build towns, villages and factories on the ruins where nothing was left and rapidly stabilize the people's living conditions. But we were able to overcome these difficulties and trials and win a great victory in the economic construction because we were firmly united with the masses of the people.

We have basically overcome the difficulties in socialist construction. Now the lives of our people are stable. It is true that their living standards are not yet very high. But no one in our country is hungry or in rags or wandering about without a job. Our people all work, receive free education and free medical care. This is a great victory won by our people in socialist construction.

We have laid the basis for rapidly developing the national economy and raising the people's living standards in the future.

As I have already mentioned, we have a huge army of competent cadres, we have built the foundations of a powerful heavy industry centered around the engineering industry and constructed a large number of modern light industrial factories. In particular, we have developed a strong, independent industry which is supplied by our own raw materials. We have laid the basis for the further development of stockbreeding.

All this firmly guarantees the more rapid development of our economy and a bigger rise in the people's standard of living.

Thank you for your attention. Now let me conclude my answers to your questions.

We oppose the reactionary policies of the U.S. government but we do not oppose the American people. We want to have many good friends in the United States.

On some Problems of our Party's Juche Idea and the Government of the Republic's Internal and External Policies

Answers to the Questions Raised by Journalists of the Japanese Newspaper "Mainichi Shimbun", September 17, 1972

I warmly welcome your visit to our country.

I have received your questionnaire through the Central Committee of the Journalists' Union of Korea.

Now, I would like to give brief answers to your questions.

1. *Some Problems Involved in the Idea of Juche*

You requested me to tell how the *Juche* idea originated.

In a nutshell, the idea of *Juche* means that the masters of the revolution and the work of construction are the masses of the people and that they are also the motive force of the revolution and the work of construction. In other words, one is responsible for one's own destiny and one has also the capacity for hewing out one's own destiny.

We are not the author of this idea. Every Marxist-Leninist has this idea. I have just laid a special emphasis on this idea.

How keenly the necessity of establishing *Juche* is felt and how much emphasis is laid on it may depend on people and on the social and historical backgrounds of a country.

In the course of my struggle for freedom and independence of our country I came to a firm conviction that we must and could work out our own destiny with our own efforts. Our struggle was hard and complex. We had to solve everything by ourselves and use our own heads to formulate the lines and methods of struggle as well.

Naturally, therefore, we met indescribable difficulties and had to pass through harsh trials. Through this, however, we obtained absolutely unique experience and lessons. We realized that the simple and ordinary working masses, if only they were brought to revolutionary awareness, could display a really great force and carry out the revolution by their own efforts in any adverse and arduous conditions.

Our situation was also extremely difficult right after liberation. We had had no experience of running the state or managing the economy. Our country was very backward, and it was divided into north and south. We could look nowhere for a ready-made solution to the problem of building a new country in this complex situation.

The first problem that confronted us was whether to take the road to capitalism or the road to socialism, so that we might quickly free ourselves from our wretched situation.

The road to capitalism meant preserving exploitation and oppression. This would not only prevent us from rousing the broad masses of the proletariat to the building of a new country, but would also involve the great danger of our country being again subordinated by another imperialist power. It was evident, therefore, that we could not follow the road to capitalism.

However, we could not take the road to socialism immediately. Socialism was what we needed. Subjective desire alone could not obtain it. We were faced with the immediate tasks of the democratic revolution which must be solved before going over to socialism. So we could not just imitate the socialist system.

From the outset we had to use our own brains to determine a political system that would serve the interests of the working class and other sectors of the working masses and that would be able to rally the broad masses of people. We also had to determine the way to effect democratic social reforms that might suit the specific conditions of our country. Accordingly, for agrarian reform, we went to farm villages and stayed many days with the peasants, exploring ways and means that would suit our rural situation.

Our experience showed that endeavoring to solve our problems in this way to suit our actual conditions was much better than mechanically copying foreign ways. Our post-liberation struggle for the building of a new country validated our *Juche* idea and increased our faith in it.

Then, we waged the harsh three-year war against the U.S. imperialists, and our country was reduced to ashes. This rendered our task of building socialism even more difficult.

The U.S. imperialists destroyed not only the dwelling houses and property of our workers and peasants but also the economy of the small and medium entrepreneurs and the rich peasants as well. During their socialist revolutions, other nations eliminated the capitalist and rich peasant classes by expropriating them, but we had no need to do so. Immediately after liberation we consistently pursued the policy of encouraging the economy of the small and medium entrepreneurs, who could fight side by side with the workers and peasants against imperialism. Moreover, it was necessary for us to protect national capital as at that stage our industry was not fully developed. However, since the economy of the small and medium capitalists and the rich peasants was utterly destroyed by the war, our Government had no need to take the trouble of reviving it.

Now that everything had been ravaged by the war, there was little difference between the small and medium entrepreneurs and the urban craftsmen. Everyone became a proletarian, so to speak. They had to pool their efforts and go along the road to socialism, this was the only way for them to subsist. In order to shore up their completely devastated agriculture, the peasants, too, had to do the same.

Proceeding from the Marxist-Leninist proposition that co-operation, even when it is based on primitive techniques, is far superior to private farming, and considering the actual fact that our peasants badly needed to work together to free themselves from their plight, we adopted an original method—boldly pushing ahead with the socialist transformation of agriculture before industrialization. As regards the small and medium entrepreneurs and rich peasants we also chose a unique way—drawing them into the co-operatives and remolding them on socialist lines because there was no necessity to expropriate them.

Again experience justified our Party's line of solving all problems in the interest of our people and in conformity with the specific conditions of our country without recourse to any ready-made formula or proposition.

Through this course we have been more deeply convinced that the correct stand and attitude to maintain in revolution and construction is to settle all problems in the interest of our people and in conformity with the specific conditions of our country, believing in and relying on our own strength, with the consciousness of masters of the revolution.

Our revolution has traversed and is traversing a very complicated and difficult road. Whenever we were confronted with difficulties and ordeals, we maintained the attitude of a master towards the revolution and thereby achieved glorious victories. This process made our conviction still more unshakable—a conviction that only by firmly relying on the *Juche* idea can one thoroughly adhere to the revolutionary stand of the working class and creatively apply Marxism-Leninism to the realities of one's country.

You asked me whether you may understand that the *Juche* idea is embodied as independence in politics, self-reliance in the economy and self-defense in national defense. Your understanding is quite correct.

Establishing *Juche* means taking the attitude of a master towards the revolution and construction. Since the masters of the revolution and construction are the masses of the people, they should take a responsible attitude of a master towards the revolution and construction. The attitude of a master finds expression in an independent and creative stand.

Revolution and construction are a work for the masses of the people, a work that has to be carried out by them alone. Therefore, the transformation of nature and society demands their independent position and creative activity.

Based on the interests of our people and on the interests of our revolution, our Party has always maintained a firm independent stand in mapping out all policies and lines through its own efforts and responsibly carrying out the revolution and construction on the principle of self-reliance. Our Party has always been able to win victories because it believed in the strength of the people and gave full play to their revolutionary zeal and creative activity, thus encouraging them to realize themselves all potentialities and reserves, and solve all problems arising in the revolution and construction to suit our true realities.

Adhering to the stand of master in the revolution and construction and enhancing the role as master are integrated concepts with different aspects. You may say that the independent stand is concerned with defense of the rights of the master and discharging the responsibility as such, whereas the creative stand concerns the development of the role of the people, the masters, in remaking nature and reconstructing society. In other words, the independent stand is the fundamental stand which we must maintain in the revolution and construction, and the creative stand is the fundamental method that we must apply in transforming nature and society.

To adhere to the independent stand it is most important that we fully guarantee independence in politics.

Independence is what keeps man alive. If he loses independence in society, he cannot be called a man; he differs little from an animal. We might say that socio-political life is more valuable to a man than physical life. He is a social being. If he is forsaken by society and deprived of political independence, though he seems alive, he is virtually dead as social human being. That is why the revolutionaries deem it far more honorable to die in the fight for freedom than to keep themselves alive in slavery.

Ignoring independence is tantamount to ignoring man himself. Who likes to live shackled to others? Why did people fight to overthrow the feudal system in former days and why are the working class fighting against the capitalist system today? Needless to say, working people wanted to extricate themselves from feudal slavery just as they want to free themselves from capitalist exploitation and oppression. We are fighting against imperialism in order to liberate our nation completely from its yoke and enable it to enjoy freedom as a sovereign nation. In a word, all the revolutionary struggles aim to attain freedom from either class or national subjugation; they are struggles of the people in defense of their independence. Our struggle for the building of socialism and communism, too, is, in the long run, to enable the people to extricate themselves from many forms of subjugation and lead independent and creative lives as masters of nature and society.

In order to become the master of its own destiny, a nation must have an independent government and firmly guarantee political independence. This is why the *Juche* idea should first be embodied as the principle of independence in politics.

To guarantee solid independence in politics, there must be a special guiding idea and a capacity for formulating all policies and lines solely in the interests of one's country, according to one's own judgment. The government that acts under pressure from, or instructions of, others cannot be called a genuine people's government responsible for the destiny of the people. A country with this sort of government cannot be regarded as an independent, sovereign state.

The principle of independence in politics demands complete equality and mutual respect among all nations. It opposes both subjugating others and being subjugated by others. A nation that subjugates others can never be free itself.

In strengthening the independence of the country, it is essential to strengthen self-reliance in the economy along with political independence. Without self-reliance in the economy, it is impossible to meet the people's growing material demands, and materially guarantee them a real role as master of the state and society. Economic dependence on others cannot guarantee political independence and without independent economic power, it is impossible to carry through the line of self-defense in national defense.

Self-defense and self-protection are intrinsic to the nature of man. A country must also have the means to defend itself. The line of self-defense in national defense is an essential requirement of an independent and sovereign state. While there are still imperialist aggressors, the state that has no defense power of its own to protect its sovereignty against the internal and external enemies is, in fact, not a fully independent and sovereign state.

Our Party's consistent line of independence in politics, self-reliance in the economy and self-defense in national defense has long since been proved correct and vital by our people through their revolutionary practices.

Next, I am going to say a few words about your question as to what we stress as an embodiment of the *Juche* idea in our present domestic policy.

Embodying the *Juche* idea means powerfully stepping up revolution and construction from an independent and creative stand.

The most urgent problem facing us at present in embodying the *Juche* idea in the Korean revolution is that of bringing about the independent, peaceful reunification of our country.

Our people have been fighting for a long time to rid themselves of the yoke of imperialism, but our national sovereignty is still being trampled underfoot by foreign aggressors in one half of our territory. Nothing is more urgent for our people today than driving out foreign aggressors and establishing national sovereignty throughout our country.

The south Korean rulers have been hampering the independent, peaceful reunification of the country for nearly 30 years, pursuing the policy of dependence on outside forces. Dependence on outside forces is the road to national ruin. This is a serious lesson our people have drawn for themselves from a long history of national suffering. It is also a reality we are now clearly perceiving through the misfortunes and pains of the south Korean people under the U.S. imperialist occupation. Our immediate task is to see that all the people in north and south Korea fight against outside forces in the spirit of independence and self-reliance and rise in the forceful struggle for the independent, peaceful reunification of our country. Achieving this reunification is the most important work in embodying the *Juche* idea in the Korean revolution today.

The central task before us now, to implement the *Juche* idea in the northern half of the Republic, is to free our people from tough labor by dynamically pushing ahead with the three major tasks of the technical revolution.

Our people freed from exploitation and oppression, have now the important task of emancipating themselves from arduous work.

Labor holds the most important place in people's social life. Eliminating fundamental distinctions that exist in work conditions and freeing the people from tough labor will be of great significance in making their lives more independent and creative.

In order to emancipate the people from backbreaking labor, it is imperative to push ahead with the three major tasks of the technical revolution. The three tasks we propose are designed to narrow down the distinctions between light and heavy labor, and between agricultural and industrial work, and to free our women from the heavy burdens of household chores by fully developing techniques by our own efforts. When they are carried out completely, arduous labor in town and country will be largely removed and the class difference in work between the working class and the peasantry be eliminated.

We proposed the three major tasks of the technical revolution as our goal in emancipating our people from arduous labor; we did this instead of merely referring in general terms to the development of heavy industry or light industry. This clearly testifies to our Party's consistent standpoint that economic construction or technical revolution should not be designed for its own sake but should serve as the means to provide the people with fruitful lives as the masters of the state and society. Attaching the greatest importance to people in every respect and serving them—this is precisely the requirement of the *Juche* idea.

Next, you asked me to tell about the education of our youth and children based on the *Juche* idea.

We are greatly concerned with the education of youth and children. This is because they are the reserves of our revolution who must carry forward the revolution through coming generations. Moreover, there is no more important job than that of educating and training people for the progress of society.

It is true that with no material means people can neither live nor develop. In this sense, the economy constitutes the material foundation of social life. However, this is always planned for the benefit of people and would be meaningless without them. It is also the people who create the means of living and improve living conditions. Therefore, what is most important in the development of society is training people to be more dynamic. In order to powerfully push ahead with the revolution and construction, top priority should be given to the work with men, that is, to the work of remolding men.

The basis of the *Juche* idea is that man is the master of all things and the decisive factor in everything. Remaking nature and society is also for people and it is work done by them. Man is the most precious treasure in the world and he is also the most powerful. All our work is for the people and its success depends on the way we work with them. Education is an important aspect of the work with men.

Education involves training people to be social beings, fully prepared mentally, morally and physically. In order to become social beings, they should first have sound social consciousness. If the younger generation, who were born in this revolutionary era, are not armed with revolutionary ideas and if they are ignorant of science, technique or literature and art as the men in our era of socialist construction, they cannot be called social beings.

Only when people have ideological and cultural background which they should possess as social beings, can they participate as masters in all aspects of social life and energetically accelerate the revolution and construction. This is why our Party always places greater emphasis on education than on any other work.

We regard as the core of education the implementation of the socialist pedagogical doctrine. Its basic principle lies in training people to be reliable revolutionary workers equipped with the ideology, knowledge and a strong physique that will enable them to take the role of master in the revolution and construction.

It is most important in training and educating people to remold their ideology in a revolutionary way. All human activity is determined by ideology. If a man is ideologically backward and morally degenerate, despite his excellent health, he cannot but be regarded as utterly useless and mentally disabled in our society. Therefore, our Party always directs its primary attention to remolding people's ideology in a revolutionary manner.

In the education of youth and children, we should give top priority to the work of training them in revolutionary ideas. If they hate work and do not serve the state and society, their knowledge and skills will be of no use, however excellent they may be. They must be so equipped with socialist patriotism and a revolutionary world outlook as to work for their people and homeland instead of trying to get promoted or earn money; we should see to it that whatever they learn is useful and that all children and young people grow up into a new type of men with communist moral traits, who are eager to work, protect and take good care of state and social property, and take the lead in the revolution and construction. This is the fundamental requirement of socialist pedagogy.

Today we are making great efforts to enforce universal ten-year compulsory senior-middle-school education. When this has been effected, our rising generation will grow up as an able builder of socialism, equipped with the essentials of a revolutionary world outlook, with a basic knowledge of nature and society, and more than one technical skill. This is of tremendous significance in revolutionizing and working-classizing the entire society, and advancing our socialist construction.

You requested me to give a detailed explanation of the *Juche* idea. But there is no end to it. All the policies and lines of our Party emanate from the *Juche* idea and they embody this idea. The *Juche* idea is not a theory for theory's sake; it is the guiding idea of the revolution and construction in our country that we put forth on the basis of the experiences and lessons obtained through our complicated revolutionary struggles. In our country the *Juche* idea is a stern fact of history established in all aspects of social life. To have a deep understanding of the *Juche* idea, it is necessary to make a detailed study of our Party's policy and our country's reality.

2. *On the Foreign Policy of the Government of the Republic*

You asked me what influence our foreign policy, based as it is on the *Juche* idea, has in strengthening the solidarity of the socialist countries, in the anti-imperialist struggle and in the consolidation of international democratic forces. I am going to make a few remarks on this question.

As you correctly pointed out, the Government of the Republic formulates its foreign policy on the basis of the *Juche* idea and is guided by this idea in carrying out all its external activities. In a word, our Republic firmly maintains independence in its foreign activities.

The Government of the Republic's independent foreign policy reflects the lofty aspirations of our people and the world's people. In our foreign activity we maintain the principle of increasing internationalist solidarity and co-operation, while holding fast to independence; we are promoting our friendly and cooperative relations with those countries which are friendly toward our country, be they large or small. Neither do we infringe upon the interests of other countries nor do we allow anyone to encroach upon our nation's rights and dignity, or meddle in our country's internal affairs. This foreign policy pursued by the Government of our Republic not only conforms with the interests of the revolution and construction in our country, but it is also in full accord with the interests of world revolution.

The principle of independence held by the Government of our Republic in its external activity is in no way contradicted by proletarian internationalism. There can be no internationalism without independence, and vice versa.

First of all, our Government's foreign policy based on the *Juche* idea is actively contributing to strengthening the solidarity of socialist countries.

The Government of the Republic strictly abides by the principle of independence in its relations with the socialist countries. With the principle of equality and independence we are developing our relations of friendship and co-operation with the socialist countries. And against all hues of opportunism arising within the international working-class movement, too, we are waging our struggle in conformity with the actual conditions of our country, always on the basis of our independent judgment and conviction.

We adhere to our principle based on independence particularly in our efforts to achieve unity and cohesion among the socialist countries. We maintain that all socialist countries should, first, oppose imperialism; second, support the national liberation movement in colonies and the international working-class movement; third, go on towards socialism and communism; and fourth, attain unity on the principles of non-interference in each other's internal affairs, mutual respect, equality and reciprocity. Although there exists differences of opinion among the fraternal parties and socialist countries, we continue to promote unity and wage a joint struggle in accordance with these four principles.

As for the anti-imperialist struggle, the Government of our Republic is fighting in accordance with our own beliefs and our actual situation. Internally, we define as a major revolutionary task the struggle against U.S. imperialism, the sworn enemy of our people, and in our external activities as well, we are actively battling to check and frustrate the U.S. imperialist policies of aggression and war and to defend world peace and security. Our Government regards it as its iron rule to give active support and encouragement to the struggle of the world's people against U.S. imperialism and is endeavoring to increase our solidarity with all the anti-imperialist forces.

With regard to the international democratic movement, the Government of our Republic also adheres to the principle of independence and non-interference. We are doing all we can to support and encourage the revolutionary struggle and democratic movement of the people in the world for peace and democracy, national independence and social progress. We have no intention to interfere or impose our ideas upon them.

Our Government also strives to unite with the new independent countries, and all other countries, on the five principles—respect for territorial integrity and sovereignty, non-aggression, non-interference in each other's internal affairs, equality and mutual benefit, and peaceful coexistence.

Our Party's *Juche* idea and our Government's independent foreign policy enjoy the active support and sympathy of the world's people. With each day, more and more people throughout the world are expressing sympathy with our Party's revolutionary *Juche* idea, and positively supporting the principle of independence maintained by the Government of the Republic.

Today progressive people in the world want to live in accordance with the *Juche* idea and many countries demand independence. No one wants to be subjugated by others. No nation will tolerate interference in its internal affairs and infringement upon its dignity; not only the socialist countries but also the newly independent countries oppose foreign interference and restrictions, and are taking the road to independence and self-reliance. Even capitalist countries do not want to blindly follow big powers any longer but are demanding the right of independent actions. The world's people are now demanding the *Juche* idea and many countries are on the road of independence. This is an irresistible trend of our time.

You wanted to hear our views on peace in Viet Nam and the Asian policy of U.S. imperialism in this context. I will now touch on this problem briefly.

Peace has not yet been achieved and the war is still going on in Viet Nam. This is very regrettable not only for you but also for the Asian people and the peace-loving people the world over. Particularly, the war in Viet Nam is causing great misfortunes and sufferings to its people.

It is entirely because of the crafty and vicious U.S. imperialist policy of aggression that peace has not been achieved in Viet Nam.

As you know, in recent years U.S. imperialism has repeatedly sustained great setbacks in the Viet Nam war and has undergone a serious political economic and military crisis at home and abroad. To find a way out of this dead end, U.S. imperialism produced the so-called "Nixon doctrine." This is a more crafty and insidious policy of aggression aimed at making Asians fight Asians in Asia and Africans fight Africans in Africa.

However, the "Nixon doctrine" is a stereotyped and wornout artifice which is quite infeasible. The reactionary ruling circles have long employed it to save themselves whenever they are driven into a predicament.

Above all, the "Nixon doctrine" is going bankrupt in the face of the Vietnamese people's heroic war of resistance. At present, the U.S. imperialists, while persistently furthering the plan to "Vietnamize" the war in south Viet Nam, are more viciously committing the criminal acts of blockading the coast of the Democratic Republic of Viet Nam and indiscriminately bombing its towns, villages and economic and cultural establishments. But they continue to suffer heavy military and political setbacks in the face of the heroic struggle of the Vietnamese people, who have risen as one in the battle for national salvation against U.S. aggression.

In order to ensure peace in Viet Nam, the U.S. imperialists must immediately stop their aggressive war, give up the policy of "Vietnamization" of the war and get out of south Viet Nam, taking with them their armed forces of aggression, troops of their satellites and puppets and lethal weapons. The Viet Nam question must be solved by the Vietnamese people themselves without any interference from outside forces.

The heroic Vietnamese people who are enjoying the powerful support and encouragement of the revolutionary peoples of Asia and the rest of the world will frustrate the U.S. imperialist policy of "Vietnamization" and surely win great victory in their struggle to liberate the south, defend the north and reunify the country.

Now, I would like to refer briefly to the Government of the Republic's position on the discussion of the Korean question at the UN General Assembly this year.

At present we take a fundamentally different position to that of our enemy on this matter.

As they did last year, the U.S. imperialists and south Korean rulers are employing the tactics of stalling the discussion of the Korean question at the UN General Assembly this year. They maintain that there is no need for the UN General Assembly to deal with the Korean question and its discussion must be postponed because talks have begun between the Red Cross organizations of north and south Korea and dialogues are going on between the north and south.

This assertion is quite contrary to the will of the Korean people; it is an extremely unjust assertion aimed at hampering the independent, peaceful reunification of Korea. Sinister designs are hidden in the scheme of the U.S. imperialists and south Korean rulers to put off the consideration of the Korean question at the UN General Assembly again this year, on the pretext of the partial contacts and dialogues now going on between the north and south. By putting off the discussion, the U.S. imperialists try to cover up their policy of aggression in Korea, and the south Korean rulers want to keep the U.S. imperialist aggressor troops stationed in south Korea. Therefore, the tactics of the U.S. imperialists and south Korean rulers in relation to the United Nations are totally aggressive and anti-popular.

To counter these enemy tactics, the Government of the Republic has decided to insist on the discussion of the Korean question at this year's UN General Assembly session.

We consider the United Nations should help the Korean people's struggle for the independent, peaceful reunification of their country because dialogues are being held between the north and south, the talks are going on between the Red Cross organizations of north and south Korea, and the north and south made a joint statement which calls for the unity of the Korean nation to reunify the country peacefully free from foreign interference.

If the United Nations wants to help toward the independent, peaceful reunification of Korea, it should not postpone but conduct the discussion of the Korean question at this year's UN General Assembly session. It should take positive steps in order that the Korean people's struggle to reunify their country peacefully on the principle of national self-determination may succeed.

The United Nations must first dissolve the "UN Commission for the Unification and Rehabilitation of Korea," take the cap of "UN forces" off the U.S. imperialist aggressor army occupying south Korea under the UN signboard and force them to withdraw from south Korea. At the same time, it must revoke all the resolutions and actions against the Korean people's struggle for national reunification, and adopt a resolution for the independent, peaceful reunification of Korea. If the United Nations takes these measures, Korea's peaceful reunification will stand a better chance of coming about.

Many countries are supporting our policy toward the United Nations today. More and more countries will give support to our just policy in the future.

We consider that with the active support of the world's progressive people, the United Nations will, sooner or later, take positive measures for the independent, peaceful reunification of Korea.

3. On the Question of the Peaceful Reunification of Korea

It is the invariable policy of our Party and the Government of the Republic to reunify the divided country independently and peacefully. From the first days of our country's division, we have made every sincere effort for its peaceful reunification.

However, our country still remains divided into the north and south; it has not been reunified though 27 years have passed since liberation. Our people who are suffering from territorial division and a national split unanimously want the peaceful reunification of the country.

The aspiration for peaceful national reunification is rising rapidly, not only among the people in the northern half of the Republic, but among the south Korean people.

When the sentiments for peaceful reunification were rapidly mounting among the south Korean people, we declared in the August 6 speech last year that we were ready to come in contact, at any time, with all political parties, including the Democratic Republican Party, social organizations and individual personages in south Korea.

After we made this new proposal expressing our readiness to get in contact even with the Democratic Republican Party of south Korea, the south Korean people increased their pressure and the world raised its voice for such a contact. This compelled the south Korean authorities to propose to hold north-south Red Cross talks and start a movement to search for families. Needless to say, we had proposed political negotiations with the south Korean side. But since we have consistently desired to have north-south contact ever since right after liberation, we valued their proposal despite its limitations and agreed to hold talks, though confined to a movement to search for families. As a result, the preliminary talks between the Red Cross organizations of the north and south opened on September 20 last year.

When the preliminary talks opened, the south Korean people, to say nothing of the people in the northern half of the Republic, deeply rejoiced over the materialization of north-south contacts and warmly hailed it with great excitement. Following the preliminary talks between the Red Cross organizations of the north and south, the sentiments for peaceful reunification mounted still higher among the south Korean people.

Scared by the south Korean people's fast-mounting sentiments for peaceful reunification, the south Korean authorities proclaimed a "state of emergency" under the fictitious pretext of "threat of southward aggression from the north" and launched the racket of suppressing the people. The declaration of the "state of emergency" by the south Korean rulers was merely a deceptive maneuver to dampen the sentiments for peaceful reunification and the democratic aspiration rapidly growing among the south Korean people.

Even after they declared the "state of emergency," we put forward different positive proposals for reunification, out of the desire to dispel the dark clouds of the national split and reunify the country in a peaceful way.

The pressure of the south Korean people, and the strong opinion of the people of the world, forced the south Korean authorities to propose secret north-south high-level talks separately from the preliminary talks between the Red Cross organizations of the north and south. Thus, as is known to the world, the north-south high-level talks were held and the North-South Joint Statement was made public with our three principles of national reunification as its main content.

The high-level talks between the north and south and the North-South Joint Statement have opened up a bright prospect for our nation in its struggle to bring about the independent, peaceful reunification of the country. The spirit of the North-South Joint Statement on the peaceful reunification of the country by the efforts of the Koreans themselves, free from foreign interference, has evoked the sympathy of all the Korean people, and the world at large.

However, the announcement of the North-South Joint Statement does not mean that all problems of national reunification will be solved easily. In order to achieve the independent, peaceful reunification of the country, all the Korean people must carry on their consistent struggle with patience.

After the joint statement was made, the south Korean authorities turned their backs and are now employing a double dealing tactic; they are not honestly implementing the agreements stipulated in the joint statement. They say good words when they have face-to-face talks with us. But as soon as they turn on their heels, they slander us and become engrossed in statements and acts contrary to the fundamental spirit of the joint statement.

The first principle of national reunification made clear in the North-South Joint Statement is to reunify the country independently on the principle of national self-determination, without relying on outside forces or their interference. Frankly speaking, reunifying the country independently means forcing U.S. imperialism out of south Korea and preventing other foreign forces from interfering in the reunification of our country.

We are in alliance with the Soviet Union and China, but they do not meddle in the internal affairs of our country. There are neither Soviet troops nor Chinese People's Volunteers in our country. The outside forces now encroaching upon our sovereignty and standing in the way of our national reunification are none other than U.S. imperialism and some Japanese reactionaries. In order to reunify the country independently, therefore, we must oppose U.S. imperialism and Japanese militarism, which are interfering in the internal affairs of our country.

Nevertheless, the south Korean authorities, even after they agreed to the principle of independent national reunification, are still making absurd allegations that the United Nations is not an outside force, that U.S. troops should remain in south Korea for a long time or that Korea should be reunified through UN-supervised elections.

The North-South Joint Statement also affirms the principle that national reunification should be attained by peaceful means, without recourse to force of arms against each other. If this principle is to be observed, both sides must refrain from words and deeds that would aggravate the situation.

We have clearly stated more than once that we have no intention to "invade the south." But the south Korean rulers say that they cannot trust our statements, and they are clamoring that they must "build up strength" for north-south confrontation by reinforcing military installations both at the front and in the rear and speeding up modernization of armaments. They are also staging military exercises more frequently. This is a grave act that will aggravate tension between the north and south.

The south Korean rulers' preposterous vilifications and provocations against us are evoking resentment among our people and People's Army and creating a tension within the dialogue after all. This act will only help produce an atmosphere of war rather than an atmosphere of reunification.

Another major principle of national reunification clarified in the North-South Joint Statement is that of promoting the great unity of the nation transcending the differences in ideology, ideal and social system.

If we do not force the socialist system of the northern half upon south Korea and the south Korean authorities do not force us to restore the capitalist system, why should we, one and the same nation, fight against each other? We are not forcing socialism upon south Korea. What society south Korea will be in the future, will be decided by the south Korean people according to their own will. The south Korean rulers are now clamoring that a "wind of freedom" should be sent into the north. This arrogant attitude is aimed at obstructing peaceful reunification.

The principle of achieving the great national unity transcending the differences in ideology, ideal and social system demands the democratization of society and the freedom of political activities for all parties, all groupings and personages of all strata. Only when society is democratized, can all the forces desirous of the independent, peaceful reunification of the country be united in one, irrespective of the differences in ideas, political views, religious beliefs and political groupings.

Even after the announcement of the North-South Joint Statement, however, the south Korean authorities have been suppressing democratic freedom as ever and intensifying their fascist repression of the people, claiming that there is no reason to revise the "Anti-Communist Law" and the "National Security Law." They are even restricting the activities of the opposition, and are preventing the opposition party members from making contact with us. They are arresting and imprisoning many people who advocated contact and interchange between the north and south and national reunification on charges of violating the "Anti-Communist Law." Some time ago the south Korean authorities went so far as to execute the patriots who had striven for democracy and peaceful reunification in south Korea. This is a naked provocation to us.

Though they solemnly pledged the nation to conscientiously carry out the agreements in the joint statement, the south Korean rulers are thus violating them without hesitation. They do not think of the consequences of their treachery to the nation.

These provocative acts of the south Korean authorities are

infuriating the entire Korean people, and the world's people as well. For the sake of national reunification we are restraining our indignation and showing patience to the arrogant gangsterism on the part of the south Korean rulers. Their acts will, in the long run, evoke greater wrath among all the Korean people.

If the south Korean authorities desist from such acts, observe the provisions of the North-South Joint Statement, the main content of which is the three principles of national reunification, make efforts to remove distrust and achieve mutual understanding, and make sincere efforts for the solution of the reunification question, we will continue to work patiently for the independent, peaceful reunification of the country.

First of all, we will exert every effort to bring about the earliest possible success of the talks between the Red Cross organizations of the north and south now going on amid the expectations of the whole nation. In this way we intend to alleviate the misfortunes and hardships of the families and relatives separated in the north and south by the artificial division of the country, and provide favorable conditions for the independent, peaceful reunification of the country.

Along with this, we will form and operate the North-South Coordination Commission as soon as possible, in order to implement the provisions of the North-South Joint Statement and so solve various problems to expedite the country's reunification.

However, the question of the country's reunification cannot be fully solved merely through contacts and negotiations in such a limited scope as the north-south Red Cross talks and the North-South Coordination Commission. The reunification of the country involves many problems which cannot be solved within the functions of the north-south Red Cross talks or the North-South Coordination Commission. To settle fundamental problems for the country's reunification, it is necessary to have contacts and negotiations on a wider scale, and in many more fields, to discuss a number of specific measures for removing the long-accumulated misunderstanding and mistrust between the north and south, promoting understanding and attaining independent, peaceful reunification. That is why we insist on immediately holding political negotiations, such as a joint conference on political parties and social organizations in north and south Korea, or a conference of the north and south Korean authorities, or a joint conference of our Supreme People's Assembly deputies and the south Korean "national assemblymen."

In order to attain the peaceful reunification of the country as early as possible, we deem it necessary to institute a north-south Confederation for the present.

The north-south Confederation we propose, involves the formation of a Supreme National Council with representatives of the Government of the Democratic People's Republic of Korea and the "Government of the Republic of Korea" to solve political, economic, military and cultural problems arising between the north and south and thereby attain national unity, while maintaining the present political systems of the north and south as they are. There is the difference in system between them. But if both the north and south abide by the principle of not forcing their social systems on each other, there will be no reasons why they should not institute a north-south Confederation.

Once the Confederation is established, there will be more contacts and visits and economic and cultural intercourses will also be effected more smoothly between the north and south. If the north and south economically work together and conduct interchange it will be possible to rapidly improve the economic situation of south Korea by utilizing the developed heavy industry and rich underground resources in the northern half of the Republic and it will greatly benefit the people in both parts of Korea. Sportsmen and artists may visit the north and south having sports games and giving art performances, and form single north-south teams and single art troupes to participate in international sports competitions and international arts festivals. Journalists may also freely travel for news coverage; and it will be possible to set up press centers of newspaper bureaus in Pyongyang and Seoul and exchange newspapers and journals between the north and south.

If a north-south Confederation is instituted and broad intercourses and visits are effected in economic, cultural and all other domains, mistrust and cold feeling between the north and south will be removed and a climate of mutual understanding and trust be created, and national unity can be easily attained. If an atmosphere of trust is created and national unity achieved between the north and south, the independent, peaceful reunification of the country will be actualized by way of establishing an all-Korea unified government through north-south general elections on a democratic basis, without any interference of outside forces.

4. On the Relations Between Korea and Japan

As you know, in those days of the Sato Cabinet, the Japanese government pursued an extremely hostile policy toward our country. But there is an indication that the present Tanaka Cabinet is pursuing a little less hostile policy than the Sato Cabinet. Sato obdurately opposed the travels of Korean citizens in Japan to and from the homeland and their trips abroad. Korean citizens in Japan are now allowed to make trips abroad to some extent and they are permitted to visit their homeland, though partially. I think this is a good thing.

However, we cannot say that everything has been settled in the relations between Korea and Japan. Many problems have yet to be solved in order to normalize relations between the two countries.

To form a friendly relationship and establish normal diplomatic relations between Korea and Japan, the Japanese government must first change its attitude toward our country. It is entirely because of the hostile policy of the Japanese government that friendly relations have not been formed till today between Korea and Japan. If the Japanese government stops meddling in the internal affairs of the Korean peninsula and takes a friendly attitude toward our country, everything will be settled smoothly between Korea and Japan.

Our position on the question of Korea-Japan relations is consistent. From the first days, the Democratic People's Republic of Korea has hoped to have good-neighbor relations with Japan even though its social system differs from ours. Even now, we want to put an end to the abnormal situation between the two countries as early as practicable and establish normal relations.

If the Japanese government is desirous of establishing good-neighbor relations with our country, it should renounce the one-sided policy and adopt an unbiased policy devoid of aggressive aim to both the north and south of the Korean peninsula; and by doing so, it should help toward accelerating Korean reunification.

Pursuing the one-sided policy, the Japanese government is trying to sow the seed of discord in the Korean peninsula by egging on one side to oppose the other. This is most undesirable. The Japanese government should hope that the Korean peninsula, its neighbor, will become stable, and north and south Korea will be reunified and live in peace and happiness. If people in the next-door house were in turmoil and fighting each other, it would not benefit Japan either, would it? We consider that for its own benefit, too, the Japanese government should pursue a friendly policy toward our country, its neighbor.

It is true that there is a difference in the systems of our country and Japan. But we think that it would be quite correct for the Japanese government to treat our country on an equal footing and establish diplomatic relations with us on the five principles of peaceful coexistence, since it has established diplomatic relations with other countries with different social systems.

Even before the establishment of diplomatic relations with Japan, we are ready to effect frequent visits of journalists, technicians and other sectors of people and conduct broad economic and cultural interchange. This sort of intercourse must not be one-sided; it must be conducted on the principles of equality and mutual benefit.

As you know, Korea and Japan are conducting some interchange at present. However, it cannot but assume a one-sided character because of the unfriendly attitude of the Japanese government. Take the exchange of journalists for example. You Japanese journalists can visit our country but our journalists cannot visit Japan. As long as this one-sided intercourse is conducted, friendly relations will never develop between the two countries.

In our opinion, whether good-neighbor relations will be established between Korea and Japan or not depends entirely on the Japanese government's attitude, aside from specific procedures.

In the establishment of friendly relations between Korea and Japan it is very important that the Japanese government guarantees the Korean citizens in Japan their national rights.

Foreigners should be guaranteed their national rights. This is the requirement of international law. But the Korean citizens in Japan are not given a treatment due to foreigners today although they have the nationality of the Democratic People's Republic of Korea. This is another expression of the Japanese government's unfriendly attitude toward our country.

We demand that, first of all, the Korean citizens in Japan be guaranteed the full right to national education, as well as the right to repatriation, and the freedom to travel to and from the homeland.

You said that Japan has incurred widespread criticism internationally by its rapid economic development in recent years and asked for our views of Japan's present situation and foreign policy. Let me make a brief remark on this point.

We do not think ill of Japan's economic development. Why should we think ill of our neighbor's economic development? If the development of Japan's economy is not used for the revival of militarism and aggression on other countries and contributes to enhancing the material and cultural living standards of the Japanese people and promoting its friendly relations with other countries, it will indeed be a good thing.

In the past, however, the reactionary Japanese ruling circles craftily schemed to speed up the militarization of the country and invade other countries on the basis of revival of Japan's monopoly capital and the establishment of its ruling system. The Japanese reactionaries have not yet dispatched troops abroad, but are laying a stepping stone for their future military aggression in other countries. This shows the danger of the revival of Japanese militarism.

At present, the Japanese reactionaries, actively speeding up the militarization of the country, have made no scruple of embarking on the road of aggression against other countries, under the guise of being their "helper." Taking advantage of the economic difficulties of some countries in Southeast Asia, they try to seize the key branches of their economy by increasing the export of capital to these countries under various names such as "government loan," "direct investment" and "joint enterprise."

They attach big political strings to their "economic aid" in an attempt to sway some new independent countries to the right and deflect them from an anti-imperialist front.

Japan's reactionary ruling circles started their full scale economic infiltration into south Korea after manufacturing the criminal "ROK-Japan treaty." They are frantically working to reduce south Korea again into Japan's exclusive colony, stepping up political and military infiltration along with the economic infiltration.

It was reported that some time ago the Japanese authorities went to Seoul and held the "ROK-Japan ministerial conference" with the south Korean rulers, at which they agreed to conclude an "agreement on industrial ownership" with the south Korean reactionaries as a price of the so-called "aid." This is also an open act of aggression designed to subordinate south Korea to Japan economically. The conclusion of the "agreement on industrial ownership" between Japan and south Korea will enable the Japanese monopolies to have privileges in their business activities in south Korea, and will shackle the south Korean economy more tightly to the rapacious Japanese monopoly capital. This will create the danger of another Japanese invasion of south Korea, just as the Japanese imperialists invaded our country in 1894 under the pretext of protecting the Japanese property and the Japanese residents. As you see, Japanese monopoly capital is paving the way for overseas aggression of Japanese militarism.

This is why our people are becoming more vigilant against the fattening Japanese monopoly capital and resolutely fighting against the militarization of Japan's economy, and its overseas aggression.

The Japanese reactionaries must not forget the lesson of history and must stop the militarization of Japan's economy and maneuvers for overseas aggression. If the Japanese reaction-aries continue to take the road of overseas aggression, oblivious of the lesson of history, they will sustain another shameful defeat in face of the struggle of our people and the world's progressive people.

The Korean people express solidarity with the Japanese people in their righteous struggle against the revival of Japanese militarism and the Japanese reactionaries' aggressive maneuvers.

I take this opportunity to send my greetings to the Japanese people and progressive men of the Japanese press who are help-ing the Korean citizens in Japan in their struggle to defend their democratic, national rights and actively supporting our people's struggle for the independent, peaceful reunification of the country.

Let us Prevent a National Split and Reunify the Country [Excerpt]

Speech at the Pyongyang Mass Rally to Welcome the Party and Government Delegation of the Czechoslovak Socialist Republic, June 23, 1973

Comrades and friends, today the international situation is developing in favor of socialism and the revolutionary forces and to the disadvantage of imperialism and the reactionary forces.

In the face of the growing forces of socialism and the national liberation, working-class and democratic movements, imperialism is on the decline and is finding itself in a more difficult situation with each passing day. In an attempt to find a way out, the imperialists are resorting to craftier double-dealing tactics.

The United States is carrying on aggressive and interventionist activities in many parts of the world under the signboard of "peace," and trying to maintain its colonial domination by suppressing small nations by force while improving its relations with big ones.

This is fully proved by the U.S. maneuverings of aggression and intervention against Korea, Cambodia, Viet Nam, Laos, a number of Arab countries, Cuba and many other nations of the world.

The United States wants to take hold of south Korea forever, as a major stronghold to save its colonial ruling system which is going into total bankruptcy in Asia.

Adopting the double-faced tactics under the "Nixon doctrine," the United States is not willing to desist from its maneuverings to instigate south Korea's bellicose elements to make Koreans fight Koreans, perpetuate the division of Korea and create two Koreas, even after the North-South Joint Statement was made public and the dialogue started between the two parts of Korea.

In step with these U.S. machinations, the south Korean authorities are also employing double-dealing tactics. They are scheming to perpetuate the division of the nation and exerting all efforts to reinforce their military strength, putting up the signboard of "peaceful reunification" on the one hand and, on the other, openly clamoring for "confrontation with dialogue," "competition with dialogue" and "coexistence with dialogue."

Because of all this the dialogue between the north and south of Korea is not making progress the way it should and a big stumbling block still lies in the way to reunification, despite the consistent, sincere efforts of our Party and the Government of our Republic for the country's independent, peaceful reunification. Consequently the bright prospect for national reunification which was opened before our nation when the historic North-South Joint Statement was published a year ago is being blighted.

Out of our earnest desire to get over the difficult situation created today and materialize the people's long-cherished aspiration for peaceful national reunification as soon as possible, we hereby reaffirm before the world the policy of our Party and the Government of our Republic for independent, peaceful reunification:

1. To improve the present relations between the north and south of Korea and accelerate the peaceful reunification of the country, it is necessary, first of all, to eliminate military confrontation and ease tension between north and south.

To remove military confrontation and alleviate tension between the north and south is a matter of pressing urgency and vital importance at present in dispelling the misunderstanding and mistrust, and deepening mutual understanding and trust between the north and south, creating the atmosphere for a great national unity, ameliorating the relations between the north and south, and bringing about the peaceful reunification of the country.

The military confrontation between the north and south with huge armed forces itself constitutes not only a major factor that menaces peace in our country but also a source of misunderstanding and mistrust.

Only when this fundamental question is solved can tension and mistrust between the north and south be removed, the climate of trust be created, and all problems be settled successfully on the basis of mutual trust. It is unnatural to advocate the peaceful reunification and hold a dialogue, with a dagger in one's bosom. Unless the dagger is taken out and laid down, it is impossible to create an atmosphere of mutual trust or find satisfactory solutions to any problems, big and small, related to the country's reunification, including that of achieving the collaboration and interchange between the north and south.

Therefore, as the first step for the peaceful reunification of the country, we have more than once advanced to the south Korean authorities the five-point proposal: To cease the reinforcement of armies and arms race, make all foreign troops withdraw, reduce armed forces and armaments, stop the introduction of weapons from abroad and to conclude a peace agreement.

Nevertheless, the south Korean authorities want to put off the solution of this urgent problem and gradually solve matters of secondary importance through different stages. Actually this is intended not to increase mutual trust and promote great national unity, but to maintain and freeze the territorial division, keeping the painful wound of national partition unhealed.

If they truly desire the peaceful reunification and seek the practical solution of the reunification question, the south Korean authorities must renounce this position and take the course of removing military confrontation.

2. To improve the north-south relations and expedite the country's reunification, it is necessary to materialize many-sided collaboration and interchange between the north and the south in the political, military, diplomatic, economic and cultural fields.

The many-sided collaboration and interchange between the north and south are of tremendous importance in rejoining the severed ties of the nation and providing preconditions for reunification. Only when such collaboration and interchange are actualized, will it be possible to consolidate the peace agreement to be concluded between the north and south.

The south Korean authorities propose in words that both sides "completely open" their societies to each other, but in actual fact they are afraid of tearing down any of the barriers between the north and south and dead set against the interchange and collaboration between the two parts of the country.

The south Korean authorities are not collaborating with fellow countrymen now. In collusion with outside forces, they are bringing in foreign monopoly capital without limit to reduce the south Korean economy completely to a dependent economy. They are even spoiling our beautiful land by introducing the pollutional industries which are rejected as "rubbish" in foreign countries.

We again emphasize that if the south Korean authorities have a spark of national conscience, they should strive to develop the economy in the interests of our nation through the joint exploitation of our country's natural resources, and bring about national collaboration in all spheres.

3. In order to settle the question of the country's reunification in conformity with the will and demand of our people, it is necessary

to enable the masses of all strata in the north and south to partici-
pate in the nationwide patriotic work for national reunification.

We consider that the dialogue between the north and south for national reunification should not be confined to the authorities of the north and south, but be held on a nationwide scale.

To this end, we propose to convene a Great National Congress composed of representatives of people of all walks of life—the workers, working peasants, working intellectuals, student youths and soldiers in the north, and the workers, peasants, student youths, intellectuals, military personnel, national capitalists and petty bourgeoisie in south Korea—and the representatives of political parties and social organizations in the north and south, and comprehensively discuss and solve the question of the country's reunification at this Congress.

4. What is of great significance today in speeding up the country's reunification is to institute a north-south Confederation under the name of a single country.

It goes without saying that there may be various ways to materialize the complete reunification of the country.

Under the prevailing conditions we think that the most reasonable way for the reunification is to convene the Great National Congress and achieve national unity, and on this basis, institute the north-south Confederation, leaving the two existing social systems in the north and south as they are for the time being.

In case the north-south Confederation is instituted, it will be good to name this confederal state Confederal Republic of Koryo, after Koryo, a unitary state which once existed on our territory and was widely known to the world. This will be a good name for the state acceptable both to the north and south.

The founding of the Confederal Republic of Koryo will open up a decisive phase in preventing a national split, bringing about all-round contact and collaboration between the north and south, and in hastening the complete reunification.

5. We consider that our country should be prevented from being split into two Koreas permanently as a result of the freezing of national division and that the north and south should also work together in the field of external activity.

Of course we are developing state relations with all countries friendly to our Republic on the principle of equality and mutual benefit; but we resolutely oppose all machinations designed to make use of this to manufacture two Koreas.

We hold that the north and south should not enter the UN separately, and consider that if they want to enter the UN before the reunification of the country, they should enter it as a single state under the name of the Confederal Republic of Koryo, at least after the Confederation is set up.

But apart from the question of admission to the UN, if the Korean question is placed on its agenda for discussion, the representative of our Republic should be entitled to take part in it and speak as the party concerned.

Our people are a single people who have lived with the same culture and the same language through many centuries, and they can never live separated in two parts.

Our proposal is to remove military confrontation and ease tension between the north and south, materialize many-sided collaboration and interchange between the two parts, convene the Great National Congress composed of representatives of people of all strata and political parties and social organizations in the north and south, institute the north-south Confederation under the single name of the Confederal Republic of Koryo and enter the UN under the single name of the Confederal Republic of Koryo. When this proposal for the country's reunification is put into effect, there will be a great turning point in accomplishing the historic cause of peaceful national reunification on the principle of the North-South Joint Statement, as commonly desired by our people and the world's people.

We expect the south Korean authorities to approach this new fair proposal of ours for reunification with sincerity.

At the same time we strongly demand that the United States must look straight at the fast changing situation of today, withdraw its troops from south Korea as soon as practicable and discontinue its aggressions and interventions against our country.

If the United States thinks that it can swallow up small nations one by one, while improving its relations only with big powers, or maintain its colonial domination by propping up its minions forsaken by the people under the signboard of "anti-communism," it is gravely mistaken. Such policies of the United States will rather arouse the resistance and hatred of the majority of the world's people and hasten its ruin.

We think that now the UN should deal a blow to the United States' maneuver to justify the occupation of south Korea by its troops under the pretext of the UN "resolution."

The UN must take the "UN forces" helmets off the U.S. troops in south Korea, make them withdraw, and dissolve the "United Nations Commission for the Unification and Rehabilitation of Korea," and thus remove all obstacles it has laid to hamper the independent, peaceful reunification of Korea. This is in keeping with the trend of the present times toward independence and peace. This is demanded by the general situation of the world.

It is none other than the Japanese militarists, who are still working desperately in the international arena as the most active followers of the U.S. imperialists in their bankrupt machination to meddle in our internal affairs. We again warn the Japanese militarists that they must also look squarely at reality, give up their hostile policy against the Democratic People's Republic of Korea and desist from their crafty maneuvers to seize an opportunity to actualize their wild desire for invading south Korea again.

Answers to the Questions Raised by L'Unita, Organ of the Italian Communist Party [Excerpt]

January 29, 1974

*Q*uestion: *One year ago we heard with a great hope that an agreement was reached between the two parts of Korea on peacefully reunifying the country, free from interference of outside forces. But, later we learned that new difficulties cropped up in its way.*

Will you please tell us what these difficulties are and how they can be overcome?

Answer: In 1972 a North-South Joint Statement whose keynote is the three principles of independence, peaceful reunification and great national unity put forward by our Party, was made public in our country as a result of the dialogue held between the north and south. This was a big advance in the struggle of our people for the independent, peaceful reunification of their fatherland. The people throughout the world, to say nothing of the entire Korean people in the north and the south, rejoiced and warmly hailed it.

After the announcement of the North-South Joint Statement we made every possible effort to put it into practice and achieve national reunification as early as possible. But in this effort we ran up against a big obstacle owing to the maneuvers of the domestic and foreign splitters to perpetuate national division.

The south Korean authorities, manipulated by U.S. imperialism, scrapped the North-South Joint Statement on the day following its signature, saying that it was no more than an untrustworthy piece of paper. After that, they kept perpetrating acts totally contravening the principles of the North-South Joint Statement and turned down all the reasonable proposals we put forward to accelerate national reunification. Then, last June, they openly announced to the world a "policy" of fixing and perpetuating the national division. The south Korean authorities asserted that north and south Korea should enter the United Nations separately. This was designed, in the last analysis, to freeze the division of the nation and keep our country divided into two parts forever.

The nation-splitting maneuvers of the south Korean authorities are a product of the "two Koreas" policy of U.S. imperialism. Seeing that it was impossible to materialize their wild design to invade the northern half of the Republic and turn the whole of Korea into their colony, the U.S. imperialists brought forward the "two Koreas" policy with the sinister aim of keeping at least south Korea in their grip. At the United Nations General Assembly session last year the U.S. imperialists, together with their followers, resorted to all sorts of tricks to pass a "resolution" on "two Koreas."

The Japanese militarists most zealously follow the U.S. imperialists in their "two Koreas" plot. While stepping up their renewed invasion of south Korea, the Japanese militarists, hand in glove with the U.S. imperialists, are actively pushing ahead with the plot to create "two Koreas". It is not for nothing that some time ago a Japanese journal wrote that "the 'two Koreas' policy is a drama acted by the Pak Jung Hi regime of a U.S. script, under U.S. direction and Japanese stage management."

We consider that the road to the solution of our country's reunification question can be cleared only by smashing the "two Koreas" plot of the U.S. imperialists, the Japanese militarists and the south Korean authorities and by putting an end to foreign interference in the Korean question.

The Workers' Party of Korea and the Government of the Republic resolutely oppose any attempt to fix and perpetuate the division of our country and thoroughly reject any outside interference in the domestic affairs of our country.

Last year's session of the United Nations General Assembly, the historically first to be held with the attendance of the representative of the Democratic People's Republic of Korea, checked the "two Koreas" plot of U.S. imperialism and its lackeys, expressed support to the three principles of national reunification laid down in the North-South Joint Statement and adopted a decision on the immediate dissolution of the "United Nations Commission for the Unification and Rehabilitation of Korea," a tool of U.S. imperialism for its interference in our internal affairs. This was a welcome step which created a favorable situation for the solution of our country's reunification question and a great victory of our Party's policy of independent, peaceful reunification.

The Workers' Party of Korea and the Government of the Republic will make every possible effort as ever for smashing all attempts to perpetuate the division of our nation and hastening the independent, peaceful reunification of the fatherland.

First of all, we will actively struggle to strip the "UN forces" cap off the U.S. imperialist aggression force in south Korea, the main obstacle to the solution of Korea's reunification question, and to force it to withdraw. At the same time, we will strive to continue the dialogue between the north and the south and to realize a many-sided collaboration and interchange between them in accordance with the principles clarified in the North-South Joint Statement.

In order to continue and develop the dialogue between the north and the south, the south Korean authorities must refrain from any acts contravening the principles of the North-South Joint Statement. They are still now persisting in the maneuvers to perpetuate the national division and the policy of dependence upon outside forces. They are harshly repressing the democratic personalities and patriotic youth and students of south Korea who call for national reunification and democracy. Today such acts of the south Korean authorities constitute the chief obstacle to the dialogue between the north and the south.

If the south Korean authorities renounce their splitting stand, respect the North-South Joint Statement and make sincere efforts for its implementation, the north-south dialogue will make a successful progress.

If the south Korean authorities continue to ignore the North-South Joint Statement and follow the road which runs counter to it, the people will not pardon them. The south Korean youth, students and people, indignant at the south Korean authorities' ever more undisguised policy of fascist repression and maneuvers to perpetuate the national split and their policy of dependence upon Japan, have risen in the anti-"government" and anti-fascist struggle for democracy. For months now they have been valiantly fighting under the slogans: "Down with the Pak regime!" "Establish democracy!" and "An immediate end to dependence on Japan!" It is natural that the south Korean youth, students and people should struggle against those who, clinging to the sleeves of outside forces, betray the nation and repress the people by force.

The just, patriotic struggle of the south Korean youth, students and people will certainly be crowned with victory, and the cause of national reunification will surely be realized through the united strength of the entire Korean people.

Answers to Questons put
by the Chief Editor of the
Yugoslav Newspaper
"Vecernje Novosti"
[Excerpt]

February 22, 1974

Q*uestion:* Yugoslavia knows well and supports the consistent efforts of the Government of the Democratic People's Republic of Korea for the country's independent and peaceful reunification.

Would you please tell me of the present political situation in the context of the dialogue between the north and the south and of the prospect of Korean reunification?

Answer: As you know, as a result of the persevering efforts of our Party and the Government of the Republic for the country's independent and peaceful reunification, the dialogue started between the north and the south of Korea and in July 1972 the North-South Joint Statement was made public with the three principles of independence, peaceful reunification and great national unity as its keynote.

After the announcement of the North-South Joint Statement the Government of our Republic put forward a number of specific and reasonable proposals to translate it into practice and made all sincere efforts for the successful progress of the dialogue. However, owing to the maneuvers of the splitters within and without, the north-south dialogue has been deadlocked and great difficulties and obstacles have been laid in the way of the reunification of the fatherland.

Even after the announcement of the North-South Joint Statement the south Korean authorities, instigated by the United States, intensified war preparations and fascist repression, more stubbornly sticking to the policy of dependence on outside forces in total contravention of the principles clarified in the statement. Then, in June last year, they made public the so-called "special statement", declaring to the world a "policy" to perpetuate the division of the nation.

At the UN General Assembly last year the U.S. and Japanese reactionaries and the south Korean authorities put forward a proposal for simultaneous UN membership for "two Koreas" and employed every conceivable trick to force it through. But this scheme was completely frustrated by the just struggle of the socialist countries, non-aligned states and many other countries of the world which support our Party's policy of independent and peaceful reunification. The UN General Assembly expressed full support to the three principles of national reunification laid down in the North-South Joint Statement and adopted a resolution on the dissolution of the "United Nations Commission for the Unification and Rehabilitation of Korea," a U.S. instrument for aggression and interference in another's internal affairs. This is a great victory for the policy of our Party and the Government of the Republic for independent and peaceful reunification and a staggering defeat for those who seek the permanent division of Korea.

The south Korean authorities' maneuvers to perpetuate the division of the nation at the instigation of the imperialist forces have caused national indignation of the entire Korean people who aspire for the reunification of the fatherland and have inevitably roused them to the struggle against the splitters within and without.

Harsh as fascist repression is today, the south Korean student youth and personages of all strata are valiantly fighting to bring about the democratization of south Korean society, save the country and the people and reunify the fatherland.

We put forward the five-point proposition: to remove the military confrontation and ease the tension between the north and the south, to materialize many-sided collaboration and exchange between the north and the south, to convoke a Great National Congress comprising representatives of people of all strata, political parties and social organizations in the north and the south, to institute a north-south Confederation under the single name of the Confederal Republic of Koryo and to enter the UN under the single name—the Confederal Republic of Koryo. This is an epochal save-the-nation plan aimed at preventing the division of the nation and reunifying the fatherland.

The only obstacle to the solution of the question of our country's reunification today is the maneuvers of the splitters, within and without, to keep our nation indefinitely divided. If the question of our country's reunification is to be solved smoothly, an end must be put first to the ''two Koreas'' plot of the U.S. and Japanese reactionaries and their interference in Korea's domestic affairs and the south Korean authorities must renounce the policy of dependence on outside forces and honestly observe the principles of the North-South Joint Statement. The south Korean authorities must discontinue their fascist repression of the south Korean people who demand democracy and the country's independent and peaceful reunification and open the way for representatives of all parties, groupings and people of all strata in south Korea to participate directly in the solution of the question of reunification. Only then will the dialogue between the north and the south make smooth progress and the solution of the question of the country's reunification be quickly facilitated.

Because of foreign interference we are now going through turns and twists in the solution of the question of the country's reunification. However, we will definitively win the cause of national reunification through an indefatigable united struggle of all the north and south Korean people with the active support and encouragement of the progressive people the world over.

Availing myself of this opportunity, I would like to express my deep thanks to the Government of the Socialist Federal Republic of Yugoslavia and the Yugoslav people for their active support to the DPRK Government's policy for independent and peaceful reunificaiton and to the Korean people's struggle to put it into effect.

The Peoples of the Third World who Advance under the Uplifted Banner of Independence will Certainly Win Their Revolutionary Cause
[Excerpt]

Speech at Pyongyang Mass Rally in Welcome of Algerian President Hourari Boumedienne, March 4, 1974

In the struggle for the achievement of the country's reunification, the long-cherished desire of our nation, we have maintained all along an independent stand for solving our national problem by ourselves, decisively rejecting the attempts to rely on outside forces.

Today the Korean question, after all, boils down to the question of whether reunification or division; whether one Korea or two Koreas.

The entire Korean people are unanimous in desiring the reunification of their country.

But the great powers want the division of our country. To divide and rule is an old method of imperialism.

The U.S. imperialists and the Japanese militarists seek the

permanent division of Korea, the former to reduce south Korea to their permanent colony and military base, and the latter to take hold of south Korea as their permanent commodity market.

Huge obstacles are still lying in the way of the reunification of our country even after the publication of the July 4 North-South Joint Statement, owing to the U.S. and Japanese reactionaries' maneuvers of intervention and their stooges' treacheries to the country and nation.

In these days the nation-splitting machinations of the south Korean rulers and their provocations against the northern half of the Republic have reached a most intolerable level.

The south Korean rulers are intensifying their fascist suppression of the south Korean people as never before, arresting and imprisoning at random south Korean youths and students, conscientious intellectuals, and even religious figures on charges of demanding peaceful reunification. They are turning the whole of south Korea into a horrible prison.

In an effort to cover up their criminal acts and divert the attention of the people elsewhere, the south Korean rulers have committed such premeditated military provocations as the spy ship infiltration in the West Sea. Trying to capitalize on it, they are raising a wholesale clamor about the "threat of southward aggression" and deliberately increasing tensions between the north and the south.

It must not be overlooked that the U.S. imperialists, in step with the provocations of south Korean bellicose elements, send one high-speed, high-altitude reconnaissance plane after another into the air above the northern half of the Republic to commit espionage acts; and openly declare that they will further increase military aid to south Korea.

This ill-omened state of things in our country suggests that the splitters within and without are, in fact, leading the north-south relations back to the state before the announcement of the North-South Joint Statement and driving the situation to the brink of war.

It has become all the clearer now who in Korea is whetting the sword of aggression under the cloak of "peace" and who is seeking the perpetuation of split under the cloak of "unification."

Those who love the country and the nation should not tolerate the machinations of the U.S. and Japanese reactionaries to convert south Korea into a permanent colony, but compel the U.S. troops to get out of south Korea, thwart the Japanese militarists' invasion, and actively turn out to build a sovereign, reunified and independent Korea.

What is the use of holding the north-south dialogue, if our nation is to live divided? The north-south dialogue must be conducted, under any circumstances, for the purpose of achieving the reunification.

If the south Korean authorities really want the reunification, they should retract the "special statement" of June, 1973 advocating the membership of two Koreas for the United Nations and approach the talks for reunification in conformity with the interests of the whole nation.

They should not bring forward such a thing as a "non-aggression pact" devoid of any guarantee for peace, but accept our proposal for concluding a peace agreement.

The so-called "non-aggression pact" brought forward by the south Korean authorities some time ago is nothing but one designed to flout the nation's will on the question of reunification.

As the whole world knows, it is not the south Korean authorities but the U.S. army commander, under the mantle of the "United Nations commander," who holds the prerogative of the supreme command of the army in south Korea. It is also the U.S. imperialists who have control over the guns, rifles and all other means of war.

Under these conditions it is utterly ridiculous for the empty-handed south Korean rulers to propose to us to conclude a "non-aggression pact," leaving the U.S. imperialist aggressor forces to stay in south Korea. Their proposal is not worth discussing at all.

The continued machinations of the south Korean authorities to maintain division lead us to disbelieve that they came to the dialogue for the purpose of reunification.

That is why we think that for its peaceful solution the question of reunification of the country should not be discussed only between the authorities of the north and south, but be referred to the entire nation for discussion.

In this connection, we propose, once again, to convene a Great National Congress or a north-south political consultative conference participated in by the representatives of all political parties and public organizations and personages of all strata in the north and south, apart from the existing North-South Coordination Commission. This is the only way for realizing the reunification of Korea.

The question of Korea's reunification should be settled by the Koreans themselves; it cannot be solved for us by any big powers or any other countries.

The present situation urgently demands of us to further intensify the struggle against the splitters in order to prevent the division of the country and realize the peaceful reunification of the country.

This is a struggle to decide whether we save the country or betray it.

If the south Korean authorities reject the independent and peaceful reunification of the country and attempt to fabricate two Koreas, persistently clinging to the policy of dependence upon outside forces, they will meet their destruction, with the disgrace of traitors never to be washed off from their names.

The south Korean people are now fighting courageously for freedom and democratic rights and the independent and peaceful reunification of the country. They are not yielding to the harsh fascist suppression by the south Korean rulers.

The struggle of the south Korean people is a patriotic struggle for saving the country and the nation and reunifying the fatherland. It is a just struggle directly related to the vital interests of the nation.

That is why our Party and the Government of our Republic will always actively support the revolutionary struggle of the south Korean people with might and main.

Our support to the revolutionary struggle of the south Korean people is by no means an "interference in other's internal affairs,'' rather it is for solving, by ourselves, the internal affairs of our nation.

As one and the same nation, we regard it as our natural duty to support the revolutionary struggle of the south Korean people.

In order to remove the tensions and prevent war in Korea, the U.S. imperialists and the Japanese militarists should not defend the present south Korean authorities who are indulging in fascist repression and war provocation maneuvers but desist from their interference in the internal affairs of our country.

Our people's struggle for national reunification enjoys ever greater support and sympathy in the international arena, being an important link in the world-wide anti-imperialist national liberation struggle.

A resolution fully conforming to our five-point program of national reunification was unanimously adopted at the Fourth Summit Conference of Non-Aligned States in Algeria last year. This was convincing proof that our people's struggle for national reunification enjoyed the full support of the world's progressive people.

Under this world trend the United Nations General Assembly last year rejected the moves of the United States and the south Korean authorities for the admission of ''two Koreas'' to the United Nations, designed for perpetuation of the division of Korea and adopted a decision on dissolving the ''United Nations Commission for the Unification and Rehabilitation of Korea,'' the U.S. imperialists' tool of aggression.

This is a great victory for our people and a common victory for peace-loving people of the world.

We express the conviction that in the future, too, the peoples of socialist countries and all the progressive people of the world, including the Asian, African and Latin American peoples, will render active support to the just struggle of our people for the peaceful reunification of the fatherland. They will deal a collective blow at the wild ambition of the imperialists to split our nation, a single nation, into two parts for ever, and their stooge's treachery to the country and nation.

The Algerian Democratic and People's Republic has made

positive efforts for the victory of the righteous struggle of our people in the international arena, always regarding our cause as its own, and, especially, extended great support to us at the Summit Conference of Non-Aligned States and the 28th Session of the United Nations General Assembly.

Our people will always remember this.

Allow me to take this opportunity to express once again deep thanks to His Excellency Mr. President Houari Boumedienne and the Algerian Government and people for the unstinted support and encouragement they extend to the policy of our Party and the Government of our Republic for the independent and peaceful reunification of the country and the struggle of our people for its implementation.

Speech at the Banquet in
Honor of Prince Norodom
Sihanouk, Head of State of
Cambodia and Chairman of
the National United Front
of Kampuchea and Madam
Princess Monique Sihanouk
[Excerpt]

April 12, 1974

Today big obstacles are still lying in the way of the independent and peaceful reunification of our country owing to the
machinations of U.S. imperialism and its stooges to provoke
war and perpetuate a national split. But the situation as a whole
keeps developing in our favor and to the disadvantage of the
enemy.

In an attempt to save themselves from their catastrophic
crisis, the U.S. imperialists and the south Korean authorities are
further intensifying their fascist repression of the south Korean
people and deliberately aggravating the tension between north
and south, raising noisy "anti-communist" clamors.

This is, however, a foolish act from which they will get
nothing.

The recent new proposal advanced by the Supreme People's
Assembly of our country to conclude a peace agreement between
our Republic and the United States clearly proves that we are
making sincere efforts at all times for the peaceful solution of the
Korean question.

If the United States, as a signatory to the Korean Armistice Agreement, is really interested in the peaceful settlement of the Korean question, it should naturally accept our peaceful initiative.

If the United States does not want to have direct talks with our Republic, it would be all right with us but only if it stops all forms of interference in the internal affairs of our country and withdraws its troops from south Korea, thereby opening a way for the Koreans to independently solve the reunification question for themselves.

If the U.S. government persists in its present attitude, rejecting both this and that proposal, it will bring only greater setbacks upon itself.

In order to realize the national aspiration for the peaceful reunification of the country, the people in the northern half of the Republic are vigorously pushing ahead with great socialist constructions, holding aloft the line of our Party. At the same time the student youth and people in south Korea have valiantly turned out in struggle against fascism and for democracy.

The Korean people will surely accomplish the cause of the country's peaceful reunification with an ever increasing support and encouragement of the peace-loving countries and peoples across the whole world.

Answers to the Questions Raised by the Chief Editor of Al Sahafa, Organ of the Sudanese Government

April 25, 1974

*A*llow me first to express my thanks to you for disseminating our Party's *Juche* idea through *Al Sahafa* and actively supporting our people's revolutionary struggle for national reunification and socialist construction.

Now let me answer your questions.

You asked us whether we were convinced of our victory from the first days of our struggle against the Japanese imperialist aggressors.

From our childhood we witnessed the miserable plight of our people downtrodden by the Japanese imperialist aggressors and experienced an acute sorrow as a stateless nation.

Occupying Korea, Japanese imperialism established a most brutal and tyrannical colonial rule over our country. The Japanese imperialist aggressors robbed our country of its wealth and ruthlessly exploited our people. They wantonly trampled underfoot even our people's elementary right to live and cruelly suppressed their struggle for freedom and liberation. The bestial, outrageous aggressors of Japanese imperialism massacred our patriots and plunged the whole country into a sea of blood.

We could not just look on the bestialities perpetrated by the burglarious aggressors of Japanese imperialism and the tragic lot of our fellow countrymen who, deprived of their nation, were going in rags and hungry, maltreated and humiliated. We started our struggle with a firm determination to crush the Japanese imperialist aggressors and regain our lost homeland at all costs and save our people from distress.

Of course, we never thought that we could easily defeat the ferocious aggressors of Japanese imperialism armed to the teeth. However, from the first days of our struggle, we were deeply convinced that we could certainly defeat them and achieve the independence of the country.

We firmly believed that we would surely win, because our revolutionary cause for the people's freedom and liberation against foreign aggressors was a just one. Human history shows that the just struggle of the oppressed masses of people against exploitation and repression and for freedom and liberation is sure to win. It is a law of historical development that the aggressors and oppressors go to ruin and the popular masses emerge victorious.

From the first days of our struggle we were convinced that the master of the Korean revolution is the Korean people and, therefore, the Korean people must and can shape their destiny only by their own efforts. It was our firm creed that when the popular masses are awakened to revolutionary consciousness and closely united they can display a really great force and defeat the aggressors with their own strength in whatever unfavorable and difficult conditions and win freedom and liberation.

Our struggle against the Japanese imperialist aggressors was indescribably hard. With a firm conviction of victory, however, we vigorously waged the struggle against the Japanese imperialist aggressors, revolutionally educating and closely uniting all those who loved the country and the people—workers, peasants, youths, students, religionists, traders and manufacturers—and thereby eventually destroyed Japanese imperialism and won national liberation.

Now, on your question as to how, in a very short period of history, we could get over the consequences of colonialism and build on the debris of war an economic foundation that could meet all our domestic demands.

A dependent and very backward economy handicapped by colonial lopsidedness was handed down to our people from the old society and even this was totally destroyed in the three-year war. Under the correct leadership of the Workers' Party of Korea, our people successfully carried out the postwar rehabilitation of the national economy in a little more than three years by displaying a high degree of creative enthusiasm and patriotic devotion and brilliantly accomplished the historic task of socialist industrialization in a very brief span of time—only 14 years—through an uninterrupted dynamic struggle. As a result, our country, once a backward colonial agricultural state, has now turned into a socialist industrial state with a powerful heavy industry, a modern light industry and a developed agriculture, which can build up the people's lives and manage the economy on its own.

This great victory won by our country is the fruit of the dedicated struggle waged by the entire people to carry through the Party's line for the building of an independent national economy by giving full play to their revolutionary spirit of self-reliance.... Next, let me explain the reason why we oppose the admission of "two Koreas" to the UN.

As you know, at the UN General Assembly last year, U.S. imperialism and its followers tabled a proposal for simultaneous entry of "two Koreas" into the UN. This proposal was a product of the "two Koreas" policy which had long been pursued by the U.S. imperialists. When they failed to materialize their wild design to swallow up the whole of Korea by invading the northern half of the Republic, the U.S. imperialists came out with the "two Koreas" policy for the purpose of keeping our country divided in two forever, and maintaining south Korea at least as their military base of aggression and commodity market. The south Korean authorities are zealously following the "two Koreas" policy of the U.S. imperialists to retain even for a few more days their military fascist regime which is shaking to its very foundation.

We can never accept the proposal of the U.S. imperialists and their stooges for the simultaneous entry of "two Koreas" into the UN. If the north and south enter the UN separately before reunification, our country will remain divided forever. This is entirely counter to our people's will and desire. The permanent division of the country will spell immeasurable misfortunes and sufferings to our people and place a great obstacle to the future development of our nation.

Our people, who have lived as a homogenous nation with one culture and one language for ages, do not want the split of the nation. They only want reunification. If there are any people in our country who oppose national reunification and want division, they are a tiny handful of persons in authority, landlords and comprador capitalists in south Korea.

Ever since the country was partitioned into north and south, because of the occupation of south Korea by the U.S. imperialist aggression army, we have exerted strenuous efforts to reunify the country independently by peaceful means. Last year when the divisive maneuvers of the splitters within and without became more undisguised, we declared that the north and south must not enter the UN separately. If they are to enter it before the country is reunified, they should do so as a single state under the single national title of the Confederal Republic of Koryo, at least after a confederation is set up.

The sincere efforts of the Government of the Democratic People's Republic of Korea to achieve the independent and peaceful reunification of the country, and our policy for the entry into the UN as a single state, have won unreserved support from the progressive people the world over. Last year the UN General Assembly actively supported our three principles of national reunification, the keynote of which is independence, peaceful reunification and great national unity. Thanks to the positive efforts of the representatives of many countries, including the Sudan, it adopted a resolution on the immediate dissolution of the "United Nations Commission for the Unification and Rehabilitation of Korea," a body on the U.S. imperialist payroll and their tool of interference in our internal affairs. They completely checked and frustrated the plot for the admission of "two Koreas" to the UN woven by the U.S. imperialists and their lackeys. This again proved clearly that our firm, consistent policy for the independent and peaceful reunification of the country is entirely correct.

At the Third Session of the Fifth Supreme People's Assembly held some time ago, the Government of our Republic took another initiative to create favorable prerequisites for the achievement of the independent and peaceful reunification of the country.

In our letter sent to the U.S. Congress in the name of the Supreme People's Assembly, we proposed talks on the question of concluding a peace agreement with the United States which, among other things, will stipulate that both sides shall not invade the other side and shall discontinue arms reinforcement and the arms race, that the United States shall not meddle in Korea's internal affairs or obstruct its reunification and shall withdraw their troops occupying south Korea, and that our country shall not be made a military base or operational base of any foreign country after the withdrawal of U.S. troops.

In order to remove the tension between the north and the south and accelerate our country's independent and peaceful reunification, it is necessary today to replace the Armistice Agreement with a durable peace agreement. The Government of the Republic has made tireless efforts for the solution of this question and held dialogues with the south Korean authorities. However, they have not accepted any of our reasonable proposals but further intensified war preparations and divisive maneuvers with U.S. imperialist backing.

Facts show that the south Korean authorities have neither intention nor capacity to solve the question of concluding a peace agreement. In this situation we consider that it is most appropriate to discuss this question directly with the United States, a signatory to the Korean Armistice Agreement and the real power that is capable of guaranteeing a peace agreement.

The reasonable step we took at the recent session of the Supreme People's Assembly is warmly welcomed and supported by many countries and progressive people of the world. However, the U.S. authorities have not yet shown any positive reaction. If they eventually turn down our just proposal, they will clearly reaffirm to the world that U.S. imperialism is the most shameless aggressor who violates our people's sovereignty, hampers Korean reunification, and is the heinous enemy of peace.

As in the past so in the future, the Government of our Republic will strengthen solidarity with the socialist countries, countries of the third world and progressive people the world over. With their active support and encouragement we will carry on a tireless struggle to materialize the independent and peaceful reunification of our country.

I take this opportunity to express my deep gratitude to the Sudanese Government and people for their active support and encouragement to our Party's policy of independent and peaceful reunification and the Korean people's struggle for its implementation.

Speech Delivered at a Banquet Given at the Great Hall of the People in Peking by the Central Committee of the Communist Party of China and the State Council of the People's Republic of China in Honor of the Party and Government Delegation of the Democratic People's Republic of Korea
[Excerpt]

April 18, 1975

The tumultuous welcome overflowing with revolutionary enthusiasm accorded us today by the citizens of Peking vividly showed the beautiful picture of great friendship between Korea and China and demonstrated the invincibility of this friendship to the whole world.

No sooner had we arrived in Peking than we had a significant meeting with Comrade Mao Tse-tung and had a friendly talk with him in an amicable atmosphere.

This is an expression of particular attention to our delegation, with which I am very pleased.

Korea-China friendship is a militant friendship between class brothers based on Marxism-Leninism and proletarian internationalism; it is a noble friendship sealed in blood through the common struggle against imperialism and an immortal friendship that will endure any ordeal and will flower forever.

We are convinced that our visit to China will contribute greatly to developing the traditional relations of friendship and cooperation between our two Parties, two countries and two peoples onto a higher plane in conformity with the trend of the development of the present era, and to accelerating the revolutionary movements in Asia and the rest of the world.

Our present era is characterized by the ceaseless struggle between the old forces and the new-emerging forces; it is a new historic era in which the general crisis of imperialism is being aggravated and the peoples of the socialist countries and the third world have appeared on the international arena as its masters.

As the economic crisis is worsening and the political crisis and social contradictions are growing acute in the capitalist world, the imperialists are more stubbornly persisting in the policy of war, threat and blackmail in an attempt to find a way out. On the other hand, the anti-imperialist struggle of the peoples of the socialist countries and the third world and the international working class is surging high on a worldwide scale.

At the present stage in which the struggle between the revolutionary and the counter-revolutionary forces is becoming increasingly fierce on the international scene, it is of very great importance to intensify the anti-imperialist common struggle of our two peoples.

We shall take this opportunity to have an ample exchange of views with Chinese comrades on problems of the development of the present international relations and take effective measures for our two peoples' future common struggle to cope with the fast changing situation.

Joining hands firmly from long ago, the Korean and Chinese peoples have been hewing out the road to national liberation and class emancipation, to socialist revolution and construction; and through their own experience they have realized that their destinies are inseparably related to each other as teeth to lips.

In the past our two peoples fought in firm unity, and defeated Japanese imperialism and also repulsed the U.S. imperialist aggressors.

In the future, too, the two peoples, as comrades-in-arms and as brothers, will fight together to victory.

The present situation in our two countries is excellent and their might is increasing as never before.

Under the leadership of Comrade Mao Tse-tung and the Communist Party of China headed by him the fraternal Chinese people have achieved great successes in the socialist revolution and construction with the revolutionary spirit of independence, sovereignty and self-reliance and converted backward old China into socialist new China in a short span of time.

The imperialists' policy of blockading and isolating China has been bankrupted shamefully, and the People's Republic of China has grown in strength as a powerful anti-imperialist revolutionary force in Asia and its international prestige is rising as never before.

In recent years in China the great proletarian cultural revolution and the movement to criticize Lin Piao and Confucius have consolidated the proletarian dictatorship, strengthened the unity of the entire people, built up the nation's economic might and defense capabilities and further renewed the people's mental and moral qualities.

Indeed, the Chinese people are now entering an era of national prosperity China has never known in its history of thousands of years.

China was historically plagued by poverty and hunger; it is inhabited by a huge population. But it has successfully solved the problems of food, clothing and housing for its people, reaping a bumper harvest every year when the world is swept by food crisis; though once far removed from modern technological civilization, it has rapidly developed its economy, culture, science and technology to such a level as to launch artificial earth satellites. All this was possible only in the present era led by the Communist Party of China.

All the epochal changes brought about in China today are the brilliant fruits borne of the long, indomitable revolutionary activities and wise leadership of Comrade Mao Tse-tung who founded the Communist Party of China and has invariably led it along the road to victory and who has dedicated his all to the freedom and happiness of the Chinese people; they are borne of his revolutionary line which has creatively applied the universal truth of Marxism-Leninism to the concrete realities of the Chinese revolution.

The Korean people warmly congratulate the fraternal Chinese people on their successes achieved in the revolution and construction, regarding them as a common victory for the world's revolutionary people.

The Tenth Congress of the Communist Party of China and the First Session of the Fourth National People's Congress of the People's Republic of China showed that the unity of the Party, the state, the people and the army in China has reached new heights and been further consolidated under the banner of proletarian dictatorship.

We sincerely wish the fraternal Chinese people ever greater victories in their future struggle to build China into a mighty modern socialist state and in their cause of liberation of Taiwan and reunification of all China.

Since national liberation the Korean people have implemented the revolutionary line of independence, self-support and self-defense in the northern half of the Republic under our Party's leadership, and thereby turned, in a short space of time, their once backward country into a strong socialist sovereign and independent state which never vacillates in whatever storm and stress.

At present our people are further speeding up the Chollima advance in order to fulfill the Six-Year Plan set forth at the Fifth Party Congress ahead of schedule this year which will mark the 30th anniversary of the founding of the Workers' Party of Korea.

As the socialist construction has entered a higher stage and the revolutionization and working-classization of the whole society is accelerated through the intensified ideological revolution in our country, the socialist economic construction goes on more successfully and there is a fresh upswing throughout all its spheres.

The successful building of socialism in Korea and China and the militant unity of the two peoples are precisely a powerful factor that will strengthen the world's socialist forces and the anti-imperialist national liberation forces and hasten the destruction of the imperialist forces of aggression in Asia.

Dear comrades and friends,

A great revolutionary transformation has taken place in the East and the look of Asia has radically changed since the Second World War.

The colonial Asia, the underdeveloped East of yesterday, has disappeared once and for all and new Asia has been born that advances toward independence, progress and prosperity.

The U.S. imperialists started going downhill after their ignominious military defeat in the Korean war and have sustained repeated setbacks in their aggressive wars in Indochina, and their hostile policy towards China has gone bankrupt. All this proves that no desperate maneuvering on the part of the imperialists can block the liberation struggle of the peoples or stop the victorious advance of socialism.

Nowadays the U.S. imperialists are again being dealt fatal blows and are sliding into an inextricable quagmire of ruin in Indochina. Yesterday the National Liberation People's Armed Forces of Cambodia defeated the traitorous Lon Nol clique, the stooges of U.S. imperialism, and finally liberated Phnom Penh.

This is a great victory won by the patriotic Cambodian people in their five-year-long heroic struggle against U.S. aggression and for national salvation, and it is another shameful defeat sustained by the U.S. imperialists in Asia.

This glorious victory of the Cambodian people over U.S. imperialism and its stooges is an important contribution to the anti-imperialist national liberation struggle of the oppressed nations and a historic event that will exert a great influence upon the development of the situation of Southeast Asia as a whole.

Availing myself of this opportunity, I warmly congratulate the National Liberation People's Armed Forces of Cambodia on their shining victories in the operation to liberate Phnom Penh and in the cause of liberation of the whole country under the leadership of the National United Front of Kampuchea with Head of State of Cambodia Samdech Norodom Sihanouk as its Chairman and the Royal Government of National Union of Cambodia.

Now in South Viet Nam, too, the Saigon puppet clique is being dealt strong punitive attacks by the South Vietnamese people and the People's Liberation Armed Forces and it is on the verge of collapse.

In Asia the imperialists have resorted to various methods and tricks one after the other such as direct armed intervention, neo-colonialist rule through their puppets and the "New Asia Policy" to make Asians fight among themselves; however, they have been unable to save themselves from doom and reached such a dead end that they can no longer hold out in Asia.

We actively support the struggle of the Indochinese peoples against U.S. imperialism and its lackeys and the anti-imperialist national liberation struggle of all the Asian peoples.

We strongly support the Arab peoples in their struggle to regain the occupied Arab territories and restore the national rights of the Palestinian people and manifest firm solidarity with the African and Latin American peoples in their anti-imperialist, anti-colonialist struggle.

Africa, which was called dark continent yesterday, is turning into a new continent over which the light of complete liberation is dawning; in Latin America, too, the colonial system of imperialism is being shaken to its very foundation.

At present the struggle of the third world peoples is developing in depth, into a collective, joint struggle to achieve complete economic emancipation, while consolidating their political independence already achieved, to destroy the old international economic order set up by the imperialists and establish a new international order.

Because of the community of their past situations and the identity of their present struggles the Korean people are standing firm by the third world peoples on the same front and fighting in close coordination with them.

Indeed, the world has never undergone such a rapid change in such depth and width as today.

The third world which emerged out of struggle is a mighty anti-imperialist revolutionary force of our times; it is a great motive power that advances the history of mankind.

The common struggle waged by the third world, which is inhabited by the overwhelming majority of the world's population and has a vast territory and inexhaustible natural resources, is a great struggle that will cut off the lifeline of world imperialism.

Once old and new colonialism is wiped out of Asia, Africa and Latin America, neither imperialist Western Europe nor imperialist North America will be able to exist.

However, this does not mean that imperialism will recede from its position of its own accord.

The further the imperialists are driven into a predicament, the more they resort to double-faced tactics, holding an olive branch in one hand and wielding a bayonet in the other and the more viciously they maneuver for aggression and war under the signboard of "peace." This is a rule.

Now the imperialists are openly working to find a way out of their deepening economic crisis in a new adventurous war of aggression.

However, war will never bring them any way out.

As historical facts show, in former days aggressive wars ended in the defeat of imperialists. Now, if they provoke war again, it will accelerate the final ruin of imperialism.

We shall always keep a sharp vigilance against the imperialist threat of war and get ourselves firmly prepared to meet the forthcoming great revolutionary event victoriously, whether there will be war or revolution.

We consider that in order to defeat imperialism, maintain and consolidate peace and hasten our revolutionary victory, we must thoroughly frustrate the counter-revolutionary double-faced tactics of the imperialists by countering the enemy's spear with our spear and meeting his deceptive "peace" tactics with our revolutionary principle.

The world's anti-imperialist revolutionary forces will definitively defeat imperialism and win final revolutionary victory, if they are strongly united and administer successive blows at imperialism and bring pressure to bear upon it everywhere.

Our people's present struggle to reunify their divided country is a major link in the whole chain of the anti-imperialist national-liberation struggle which is being carried out on a worldwide scale.

Now that the colonial system of imperialism is in the process of total disintegration the colonial rule of U.S. imperialism in south Korea will never remain intact, either.

Encouraged by the successful socialist construction in the northern half of the Republic, the people of all strata in south Korea are waging an increasingly dynamic struggle against fascism and for democracy, and the colonial military fascist rule of

U.S. imperialism and its stooges is sinking into a serious crisis.

In an endeavor to save themselves from crisis, U.S. imperialism and south Korea's ruling clique are intensifying their fascist repression of the south Korean people and further stepping up their preparations of war against the northern half of the Republic.

However, history is not moving as the imperialists and their lackeys expect; it is advancing steadily as the people, makers of history, wish, in the direction in which they are moving.

If the south Korean rulers continue to suppress at the point of the bayonet the people's discontent and wrath that is underlying south Korean society, it will result in a greater revolutionary explosion.

If revolution takes place in south Korea, we, as one and the same nation, will not just look at it with arms folded but will strongly support the south Korean people.

If the enemy ignites war recklessly, we shall resolutely answer it with war and completely destroy the aggressors.

In this war we will only lose the Military Demarcation Line and will gain the country's reunification.

The problem of whether there be peace or war in Korea now depends, in the last analysis, on the attitude of the U.S. which actually holds all powers in south Korea and lords it over there.

If the U.S. really desires peace in Korea and does not want to obstruct the peaceful reunification of Korea, it should stop instigating the traitorous forces rejected by the people in south Korea and it should not interfere in what the people are doing, so that they may realize the democratization of society and establish a democratic regime as they demand.

U.S. imperialism must desist from its aggressive ambition to rig up "two Koreas" and take hold of south Korea as its permanent colony and military base, and must get out of south Korea.

If U.S. troops pull out of south Korea and a democratic figure with national conscience comes into power in south Korea as its people demand, we will firmly guarantee a durable peace in Korea and successfully solve the question of Korea's reunification among us Koreans by peaceful means.

The Communist Party of China, the Government of the People's Republic of China and the Chinese people always give firm support and encouragement to our people in the just struggle for the country's independent and peaceful reunification.

I take this opportunity to express my profound gratitude to the Communist Party of China, the Government of the People's Republic of China and the Chinese people for having sent their volunteers to help our people with blood during the Korean war, for having given us a lot of aid in our postwar rehabilitation and reconstruction and in our work of socialist construction and for carrying on positive activities in support of our people's struggle for national reunification on the international arena.

Dear comrades and friends,

The future of the world belongs to the peoples who advance, holding aloft the banner of Marxism-Leninism, the revolutionary banner of anti-imperialist struggle.

In order to promote the common cause of anti-imperialism and achieve the final triumph of the cause of socialism, the Korean people will march forward for ever shoulder to shoulder with the fraternal Chinese people and will fight on firmly hand in hand with the peoples of the socialist countries, the third world peoples and all the progressive people of the world.

Speech Delivered at a Banquet Given at the Great Hall of the People in Peking on the Visit of the Party and Government Delegation of the Democratic People's Republic of Korea to the People's Republic of China

[Excerpt]

April 25, 1975

Through our current visit to China we have witnessed with deep impressions the brilliant successes achieved by the Chinese people in the socialist revolution and construction under the leadership of Comrade Chairman Mao Tse-tung and the Communist Party of China.

The People's Republic of China has made a leaping progress in all the political, economic, scientific, cultural, and military spheres, and its look has changed radically.

The changes taking place in China today give a great inspiration to the world's revolutionary people who are fighting for national liberation and socialism.

Our delegation rejoices over this as over our own achievement and warmly congratulates you and the entire Chinese people.

We had a memorable meeting with Comrade Chairman Mao Tse-tung; we also met with Comrade Premier Chou En-lai and held a number of serious and friendly talks with the leading comrades of the Chinese Party and Government.

During our talks we expressed our unanimous resolve to strengthen and develop the relations of friendship and cooperation between our two Parties, two countries and two peoples onto a higher plane in conformity with the present development of the situation in the struggle against imperialism and for the victory of the cause of socialism, and we reached a complete agreement of views on all matters discussed.

This visit of our delegation to China has borne good fruits, and this fully demonstrated to the whole world the invincibility of the great friendship sealed in blood between the Korean and Chinese peoples.

The strengthening of friendship and unity between the peoples of our two countries based on Marxism-Leninism and proletarian internationalism contributes greatly to speeding up socialist construction in the two countries, cementing the unity of the world's progressive people and bringing earlier the victory of the anti-imperialist revolutionary cause.

Having seen the militant friendship and unity between our two countries strengthening and developing further, the imperialists and their stooges cannot but betray their anxiety and fear now.

The results of this visit of our delegation to China will display a great vitality in the future joint struggle of the two peoples.

The present developments in Asia show more vividly than ever before that the victory of the liberation struggle of the people and the downfall of the imperialists and their lackeys are a trend of our times, which no force can check.

The Korean people will fight on for ever in firm unity with the fraternal Chinese people for the victory of the cause of peace and democracy, national independence and socialism; and will fight in unity with all the anti-imperialist revolutionary forces throughout the world.

Dear comrades and friends,

We are very much satisfied that our delegation's visit to the People's Republic of China has produced good fruits in all spheres. We are leaving your country with deep, unforgettable impressions.

On our return home, we will convey the fraternal Chinese people's warm sentiments of militant friendship towards the Korean people.

Lastly, I warmly wish the Chinese people greater successes in their struggle to strengthen proletarian dictatorship, completely eradicate the capitalist elements and turn their country into a powerful modern socialist state under the leadership of Comrade Chairman Mao Tse-tung and the Communist Party of China.

Speech Delivered at a Banquet Given at the Palace of the State Council of the Romanian Socialist Republic by Comrade Nicolae Ceausescu, General Secretary of the Romanian Communist Party and President of the Romanian Socialist Republic, and Mme. Ceausescu [Excerpt]

May 22, 1975

Since our arrival in your country today we have been accorded enthusiastic welcome and utmost hospitality by you and the citizens of Bucharest at the airport and along the streets.

The whole of Bucharest formed a sea of flowers to welcome us; huge crowds of citizens turned out to the streets to dance and sing in a joyous festive mood and gave us an exceptionally splendid and eager welcome.

We were greatly moved by this.

Your welcome and hospitality accorded us are an expression of the Romanian people's deep love and friendship toward the Korean people and a forceful demonstration of the daily strengthening and developing friendship and solidarity between our two peoples.

As class brothers fighting together against imperialism and for the victory of the cause of socialism, the Korean and Romanian peoples have long established the close ties based on Marxism-Leninism and proletarian internationalism.

Following the visit to our country in June 1971 by the Party and Government delegation of the Romanian Socialist Republic headed by Comrade Nicolae Ceausescu, the solidarity and cooperation between our two peoples developed to new heights.

There have been frequent visits between our Parties, state bodies and social organizations; our mutual support and solidarity have strengthened in political spheres and economic, technological and cultural cooperation expanded.

The excellent relations of friendship now existing between our two peoples reflect the voluntary and comradely relations of friendship among the peoples of the fraternal socialist countries based on the principles of complete equality and independence.

The industrious and courageous Romanian people have traversed the road to new civilization since their liberation from fascist yoke and, in a short span of time, they have turned their backward country into a prosperous, sovereign and independent socialist country.

The Romanian Communist Party and Government, under the leadership of Comrade Nicolae Ceausescu, their outstanding leader, are now maintaining an independent stand on problems related to the general development of the country, and in the sphere of external activity, too, are promoting relations among different countries on the basis of complete equality and independence.

The 11th Congress of the Romanian Communist Party held toward the end of last year was a congress of major importance in the struggle of the Romanian people to build a comprehensively developed socialist society and achieve an independent development of their country.

Thanks to the successes achieved by the Romanian people in carrying out internal and external policies, the international prestige of the Romanian Socialist Republic is increasing as the days go by.

We are happy that we are going to have an opportunity this time to witness the successes achieved by the fraternal Romanian people in the construction of a new society, and we wish you greater successes in your struggle.

The Korean people have implemented our Party's independent lines and policies and thus turned their country, once a backward colonial, semi-feudal society, into a socialist state with the firm foundation of independent national economy in a short span of time.

Experience tells us that if a people wants to make its country rich and strong and develop it and achieve national prosperity, it must guarantee political independence, and at the same time, realize economic self-support and maintain independence in economic construction.

In order to achieve economic self-support, they must produce for themselves what is fundamental, what is in great demand; as for what is in small demand, or in short supply or cannot be produced in their country, it should be obtained through economic interchange with other countries on the principle of meeting each other's needs.

It goes without saying that while putting main emphasis on consolidating and developing the socialist market, the socialist countries should develop economic relations with the newly independent states and, further, with the capitalist countries, too.

The socialist countries should actively conduct economic interchange with other countries, relying on the socialist market. This will not only help develop their economy in a comprehensive way and ensure their sovereignty and independence but also greatly contribute to increasing mutual understanding and promoting solidarity with various countries of the world and to maintaining and consolidating peace.

Dear comrades and friends,

It is an irresistible trend of the times that the world's people are taking the road to independence today when imperialism is going into total bankruptcy and ruin, while socialism and national liberation revolution are triumphing on a world-wide scale.

Even some capitalist countries, to say nothing of socialist countries and newly independent states, do not want to follow great powers blindly any longer but want to act independently.

Some time ago imperialist aggressors were driven out of Cambodia and South Viet Nam and their puppets collapsed. This again clearly showed that the complete fall of the colonial ruling system of imperialism in Asia, Africa and Latin America is inevitable.

The disintegration of the military fascist dictatorships in Greece and Portugal which had been aligned with international imperialism shows that in Europe, too, imperialist domination is being weakened and crumbling.

The imperialists are not only being hit from without but also from within because of acute economic crisis.

In the prevailing situation, if the peoples of socialist countries, the international working class, the national liberation movements and all progressive forces throughout the world fight in firm unity, they will be able to check and crush the imperialist policies of aggression and war with a decisively overwhelming force and hasten the victory of the cause of peace and democracy, national independence and socialism.

Today the basic trend of the development of the present era is vividly reflected also in the development of the situation in our country.

Encouraged by the successful socialist construction in the northern half of the Republic, the people in south Korea are daily intensifying their struggle for the democratization of society and the independent and peaceful reunification of the country; and the traitorous rulers are raising a hue and cry, driven deeper into a dead end.

It is a fully legitimate national aspiration that our nation, originally united, should be completely free from imperialist yoke and restore national unity.

We Communists regard it as our most important duty to strive, first of all, to solve our own national problems correctly; we consider this the way to contribute substantially to the advancement of the world communist movement.

At present some outside forces still try to divide our nation against our will and perpetuate the division; and to this end, they are propping up south Korean puppets forsaken by the people, breathing their breath into them and casting sheep's eyes at them.

In the final analysis, this will not create an atmosphere of peace in the Korean peninsula but further aggravate tension and increase the danger of war.

Nothing is done well by force; a forcible method never lasts long.

If the forces who obstruct the reunification of Korea do not want to suffer still more ignominious defeats, they should desist from the "two Koreas" plot and from their maneuvers to perpetuate the nation's division, which go against our people's national aspiration, should stop breathing their breath into south Korea's present rulers who are floundering isolated from within and without, and should withdraw from south Korea all foreign troops disguised as the "UN forces," before it is too late.

Then, peace will be preserved in Korea as the Korean people and the world's people desire.

In the future, too, we will render active support and encouragement to the south Korean people in their anti-fascist, democratic struggle for the right to live and the reunification of the country. When all foreign troops get out of south Korea and the society is democratized, we the Korean nation will successfully solve the reunification question with our own efforts.

The Romanian Communist Party and Government and people gave our people moral and material aid in the days of the Korean war and the postwar rehabilitation and construction; still today they are positively supporting and encouraging our people in the just struggle for socialist construction and the reunification of the country.

For this I would like to offer my warm thanks to Comrade Nicolae Ceausescu, the Romanian Party and Government and the fraternal Romanian people.

Dear comrades and friends,

It is highly important to strengthen the unity and cohesion of the socialist countries in reinforcing the world anti-imperialist forces.

We are convinced that in spite of their differences of opinion the socialist countries will be able to achieve unity on the basis of opposition to imperialism, support for the national liberation movements in colonies and the international working-class movement, continued advance towards socialism and communism and adherence to the principles of non-interference in each other's internal affairs, equality and mutual benefit.

We believe that our current visit to Romania will contribute greatly to further consolidating the traditional relations of fraternal friendship and cooperation between the Parties, Governments and peoples of our two countries and to cementing the unity and cohesion of the socialist countries and the international communist movement.

Speech Delivered at an Algiers Mass Meeting to Welcome the Party and Government Delegation of the Democratic People's Republic of Korea
[Excerpt]

May 28, 1975

We have visited the beautiful Algerian Democratic People's Republic this time, carrying with us the deep sentiments of fraternal friendship toward the Algerian people.

I would like first to express my deep thanks to the citizens of Algiers for enthusiastically welcoming us with warm militant amity here at this grand meeting.

I have been granted the title of honorary citizen of Algiers just now. This is an expression of your profound trust in us and your warm friendship for the Korean people.

I feel greatly delighted and honored to have been granted the title of honorary citizen of Algiers, the city of heroes.

At this place Your Excellency Mr. President Houari Boumedienne, our comrade-in-arms and brother, made an excellent, inspiring speech filled with special intimacy toward us.

I am grateful for this.

Availing myself of this opportunity, I would like also to convey the warmest militant greetings of the Central Committee of the Worker's Party of Korea, the Government of the Democratic People's Republic of Korea and the entire Korean people to the Council of Revolution, the National Liberation Front and the Government of Algeria and the fraternal Algerian people.

Through our current visit to Algeria we are receiving deep, indelible impressions.

We have been moved by the utmost hospitality and unbounded friendly feelings of the Algerian people towards us, their revolutionary quality and fortitude and their outstanding successes in the building of a new society.

This mass meeting of today is a vivid manifestation of the Algerian people's warm friendship and militant solidarity for the Korean people and a demonstration of firm unity among the third world peoples who are fighting side by side under the banner of independence against imperialism.

The Korean people treasure their friendship with the Algerian people that was forged in the flames of the fierce struggle against foreign imperialism and consolidated and developed through the common struggle to build new, prosperous countries under the banner of independence; it gives them a great pleasure to have such a revolutionary people as the Algerian people as their close friends on the African continent.

The Algerian people raised the first torchlight of armed struggle against colonialists in Africa. In the present struggle for the building of a new society, too, they are advancing in the van with high revolutionary zeal.

During our current visit to Algeria, we have been profoundly impressed by a new life coming into full bloom in the land of Algeria which had been reduced to debris by colonialists through their aggression and plunder.

Yesterday and today we visited a modern auto complex, the cooperativized Moudjaiya rural community, Algiers University and the Institute of the Fuel and Chemical Industries, excellent training centers for Algerian cadres, which show the might of new Algeria.

Through this visit we could realize that the Algerian people are achieving tremendous successes in the industrial, agrarian and cultural revolutions under the motto, "The revolution is carried out by the people and for the good of the people."

Through their dynamic industrial revolution the Algerian people have built many modern plants and laid the foundations of national industry.

They vigorously carried out rural construction and thus built rural villages beautifully and markedly raised the living standard of the peasants, and made much progress in the work of ensuring the coordinated development of town and country.

To eliminate the distinctions between towns and the countryside through the construction of modern rural communities is a most correct road to socialism.

The Algerian people have also made a shining success in overcoming the cultural backwardness left over by colonial rule and building a new national culture.

While firmly maintaining non-alignment policy in external spheres, the Algerian Democratic and People's Republic is actively supporting the national liberation movement of the oppressed peoples, firmly struggling for the fair solution of international questions concerning the destiny of the third world and supporting in every way the Arab people's struggle to regain the occupied Arab territories and reclaim the national rights of the Palestinian people.

Because of its splendid achievements in the building of a new society and its independent, anti-imperialist foreign policy the Algerian Democratic and People's Republic exerts a great influence on the development of international relations and its international prestige is increasing each day.

Today Your Excellency Mr. President Houari Boumedienne, the outstanding leader of the Algerian people, stands in the van of the Algerian revolution and the victories and successes of the Algerian people are guaranteed by the correct leadership of the Council of Revolution headed by you.

The correct leadership of a leader is an important guarantee for the victory of the revolutionary struggle and the work of construction.

Only when a people are led correctly by their leader, can they achieve brilliant successes in revolution and construction and follow the straight road to victory.

Your Excellency Mr. President Houari Boumedienne puts forward correct lines and policies and wisely leads the Algerian people.

Your Excellency Mr. President Houari Boumedienne's policy of carrying out the three revolutions—the industrial, agrarian and cultural—and advancing toward socialism is an important policy to further develop the Algerian revolution in depth and accelerate the building of a new society in Algeria.

The Algerian people, rallied closely around Your Excellency Mr. President Houari Boumedienne, will win greater victories in the struggle for socialist construction by thoroughly implementing revolutionary lines and policies set forth by Your Excellency Mr. President.

It is a historical inevitability that the people freed from imperialist colonial rule should take the road to socialism.

Only when the people who have achieved independence advance along the road of socialism, can they avoid the sufferings and calamities they underwent in the old society and open a short cut toward freedom, welfare and national prosperity.

Today many countries of the third world are advancing towards socialism. This shows that, after all, all nations will advance towards socialism.

The Algerian revolution reflects the process of the great resurrection of Africa.

Now the African continent is on the eve of complete liberation.

The old powers that possessed colonies in Africa have mostly been kicked out and the majority of the countries on this continent have won independence; and the racist regimes of South Africa and Rhodesia are being hit from within and without and shaken to their foundation.

We firmly believe that the African people will vigorously fight in firm unity and, thus, definitely build free and prosperous, new Africa, Africa without imperialism and colonialism.

The Middle East question is one of the international questions which must be solved quickly at the present time.

We strongly demand that in order to solve the Middle East question correctly, first of all, the aggressive maneuvers of the imperialists and Zionists in this part of the world be terminated, that the Israeli invaders withdraw from all the Arab territories occupied by them and that the national rights of the Palestinian people be reclaimed.

The African countries are acting in concert with the Arab people in the struggle against imperialism and Zionism.

This is very good and has an important bearing on hastening the victory of the common cause against imperialism.

In the future, too, the Korean people will firmly stand on the side of the Arab people battling against imperialism and Zionism and actively support and encourage the Palestinian people's struggle for the complete liberation of the country and the restoration of national rights and the Arab people's struggle to regain the occupied Arab territories and defend national dignity.

The Korean people stand firm by the third world peoples because of their common plight in the past and their common goal of struggle at present.

Now, the peoples of the third world have appeared as legitimate masters of the world; they form a great motive force that advances human history.

The appearance of the third world in the international arena as an independent political force, as a great anti-imperialist revolutionary force of our era, has opened a new, glorious epoch in the history of the Asian, African and Latin American peoples who were humiliated and oppressed before.

At present the third world peoples are actively endeavoring for their complete economic liberation, at the same time consolidating the political independence of their countries they have already achieved.

They are dynamically waging a collective, joint struggle to destroy the old international economic order fixed by the imperialists at will and establish a new international order that will conform with the will and interests of the third world peoples and the peace-loving people throughout the world, foil all the imperialist policies of plunder and blackmail and to safeguard their national sovereignty and natural resources.

The countries of the third world took a common position at the Fourth Summit Conference of Non-Aligned States and at the Special Session of the UN General Assembly on the Problem of Raw Materials and Development, the UN Conference on Sea Laws, the Conference of Developing Countries on Raw Materials, the Summit Conference of the Organization of Petroleum Exporting Countries and a number of other international conferences held later. This vividly reflected the fundamental change in the development of our time.

If the third world countries firmly unite politically and strengthen economic and technological cooperation on the principle of meeting each other's needs, they can attain their economic independence in a short period of time without being indebted to great powers and achieve the common prosperity of the third world.

When the peoples of the third world, which has the greater part of the world's population and territory and inexhaustible national resources, form a broad anti-imperialist united front and fight in close unity, it will have a decisive impact on the development of the general international situation.

Through united struggle the third world will be able to check all manner of imperialist arbitrariness in the international arena and even convert the UN into a truly peace-loving, progressive organization that will benefit the world's peace-loving people.

The policy of non-alignment occupies an important place in the struggle of the third world peoples against imperialism and colonialism and all forms of aggression and interference and for national liberation and sovereignty, peace and social progress.

The policy of non-alignment represents the trend of our time in which imperialism is falling to ruin and many countries of the world take the road of independence, calling for complete equality in international relations.

Because it reflects a wide range of demands of the development of the present time, the policy of non-alignment is uniting many countries with different social systems and displaying ever greater vitality.

The Korean people take the same stand as the third world peoples on the fundamental problems in our time, notably the problems that concern the future destiny of the third world, and firmly support the policy of non-alignment.

The principles governing the policy of non-alignment are in line with the principles of the independent home and foreign policies pursued invariably by our Party and the Government of the Republic.

Holding aloft the revolutionary banner of anti-imperialist struggle, the Korean people will continue to strengthen their solidarity with the third world countries and all other international revolutionary forces and fight staunchly to build a new world without imperialism, exploitation and oppression.

Dear comrades and friends,

The Korean people's struggle for socialist construction and the country's reunification is now making progress as part of the joint struggle of the world's peoples against imperialism.

Our people waged a long hard-fought armed struggle which culminated in crushing Japanese imperialism and liberating the fatherland. Then, under the leadership of the Workers' Party of Korea they successfully carried out democratic revolution, socialist revolution and socialist construction in a brief span of time and thus converted their underdeveloped country into a socialist country with solid foundations of an independent national economy.

We could achieve shining victories because we followed an independent policy throughout the whole course of revolution and construction.

Our own experience strongly convinces us that firmly upholding independence and building an independent national economy in the spirit of self-reliance is the shortest and most correct way to turn the once poor and backward countries into rich and strong and developed ones and make the oppressed and maltreated people strong and dignified.

Our people will, as ever, advance dynamically along the path of independence and self-support chosen by themselves and also solve the question of national reunification independently, shattering any foreign interference.

The Government and people of the Algerian Democratic and People's Republic always actively support our people's struggle for the independent and peaceful reunification of the country.

In the international arena Algeria, regarding our people's cause as its own, roundly exposes and denouces the maneuvers of the imperialists and the south Korean puppet clique to perpetuate national division.

Thanks to the concerted efforts of Your Excellency Mr. President Houari Boumedienne and leaders of many other countries of the third world, the Fourth Summit Conference of Non-Aligned States unanimously adopted a resolution which is in full accord with our five-point proposition for national reunification.

Afterwards, at the UN, too, the debate on the Korean question has progressed favorably for our people's cause of national reunification.

In the past the Korean question in the UN was handled contrary to the will and interests of our people due to the maneuvers of the imperialists. But the situation is changing these days.

Now, when the Korean question is discussed in the UN General Assembly, the representative of the Democratic People's Republic of Korea, a genuine representative of the Korean people, participates in it and makes reasonable claims for the settlement of the question of our country's reunification; as the forces of the progressive countries of the world supporting us grow, the imperialists and their lackeys find themselves in a harder situation.

In your speech at the banquet given in our honor on the day of our arrival here, Your Excellency Mr. President again voiced full support for our people's cause of national reunification and stressed that the UN should strive for the fair solution of the Korean question.

We are sure that in the future the socialist countries, the third world countries and the world's progressive forces will completely overwhelm the imperialists at the UN and that when discussing the Korean question, they will take a decisive action for the withdrawal of all foreign troops disguised as "UN forces" in south Korea, as we have been demanding.

Taking this opportunity, I would like to express my deep thanks to Your Excellency Mr. President Houari Boumedienne, the Council of Revolution, the Government and National Liberation Front of the Algerian Democratic and People's Republic and to the Algerian people for making every sincere effort to support our people in their just struggle for the independent and peaceful reunification of the country.

The Korean and Algerian peoples fought protracted, bloody struggles with arms in hand against imperialist aggressors, sincerely sympathizing with each other and supporting each other.

In the period of the liberation war when the Algerian people were waging an arduous armed warfare against foreign imperialists, our people positively supported and encouraged them in their just struggle, standing firm by the Algerian people fighting against the aggressors; when the Provisional Government of the Republic of Algeria was established, the Government of our Republic was the first to recognize it.

The friendship and solidarity forged between our two countries on the common front of anti-imperialist struggle have rapidly strengthened in recent years in all spheres on the basis of independence.

The friendship and solidarity between our two countries have developed to new heights particularly since Your Excellency Mr. President Houari Boumedienne's visit to our country last year.

We are convinced that our current visit to Algeria will be a turning point in ensuring the further efflorescence and development of the traditional friendship and cooperative relations between our two countries throughout all the political, economic and cultural spheres.

Holding high the revolutionary banner of anti-imperialist struggle, the banner of independence, the Korean people will fight forever hand in hand with the fraternal Algerian people to hasten the victory of our common cause.

Speech Delivered at a
Luncheon Given at the
Presidential Summer
Palace in Brdo by Comrade
Josip Broz Tito, Chairman
of the Yugoslav League of
Communists and President
of the Socialist Federal
Republic of Yugoslavia,
and Mme. Tito [Excerpt]

June 6, 1975

omrade Josip Broz Tito's speech we have just heard here well
expressed our two peoples' common sentiments and gave us a
great inspiration.

The peoples of Korea and Yugoslavia have brilliant
revolutionary traditions of anti-imperialist and anti-fascist armed
struggles they waged in the past and have established close ties of
friendship on the same road to win the cause of the international
working class.

The relations of friendship and cooperation between our two
peoples have entered a new age of efflorescence in recent years,
reflecting the present stage of the development of the international
communist movement in which independence is demanded, as
well as the common desire of the third world which has made its
appearance in the international arena.

We are profoundly convinced that our current visit to Yugoslavia will mark a turning point in further deepening our mutual trust and friendship and expanding and developing the friendship and solidarity between the two Parties and two countries to new heights.

We are happy to have an opportunity of witnessing the achievements recorded by the Yugoslav people in socialist construction under the wise leadership of Comrade President; particularly, we highly estimate a great constructive contribution you are making to the development of international relations by actively promoting the non-alignment policy from a firm independent stand.

The non-alignment policy reflects the trend of the development of our times in which imperialism is falling to ruin and many countries of the world are taking the road to independence; this policy holds an important place in the struggle of the third world peoples against all forms of aggression, interference, subjugation and inequality.

Because it broadly reflects the demands of the development of the present times, the non-alignment policy unites many countries with different social systems and has an increasing influence on the development of the international situation as a whole.

The principles of the non-alignment policy accord with the principles of the independent home and foreign policies invariably maintained by our Party.

Throughout the whole course of its leadership to the revolution and construction, our Party has held fast to independence and consistently adhered to the policy of solving the question of national reunification also independently by our people's own efforts, rejecting the interference of outside forces.

Basing itself on the consistent independent policy, our Party has actively supported the non-alignment policy and has regarded the struggle of the non-aligned nations as its own cause.

The adoption at the Fourth Summit Conference of Non-Aligned States of a resolution on the Korean question in full conformity with our five-point policy of national reunification indicated that the destinies of the Korean people and the non-aligned nations are inseparably linked together.

The Coordinating Bureau of the Non-Aligned States that met in Havana some time ago adopted a recommendation on admitting the Democratic People's Republic of Korea as a member of the non-aligned movement.

We are very much pleased with this and determined to wage more powerfully the anti-imperialist, anti-colonialist common struggle joining in the ranks of non-aligned nations.

As the non-aligned movement grows in scope and strength, another signal progress will be made in the struggle to demolish the old economic order arbitrarily established by the imperialists in the international arena and replace it with a new international order to meet the will and interests of the peace-loving people.

Availing myself of this opportunity, I would like to express my deep thanks to Comrade Josip Broz Tito, the Yugoslav Government and people for the efforts made by Yugoslav comrades for the admission of our country as a member of the non-aligned nations and their positive support for our people's struggle for the independent and peaceful reunification of the country.

Comrades and friends,

As the shining victories of the Cambodian and South Vietnamese peoples show, the present international situation is turning further in favor of socialism and the national liberation revolution, and imperialism is steadily declining to ruin.

This is the law of historical development which no force on earth can check.

If all the socialist countries and all the progressive forces of the world fight in close unity, imperialism can be finally liquidated and a new world free from exploitation and oppression be built.

Our people will as ever positively support and encourage the peoples of all countries in their struggle against imperialism and actively strive for the fulfillment of their national and international duties.

We greatly value the friendship and solidarity between the Korean and Yugoslav peoples based on the principles of complete equality and independence. The relations of fraternal friendship and cooperation between our two peoples will be strengthened and

developed forever through the struggle to attain the common goal
and ideal.

On the Occasion of the 30th Anniversary of the Foundation of the Workers' Party of Korea
[Excerpt]

October 9, 1975

Let Us Achieve the Independent, Peaceful Reunification of the Country

Comrades,

Reunifying our divided country is the greatest national duty and the most important revolutionary task for our Party and people.

The question of our country's reunification is essentially a question of taking back the territory and population robbed by the foreign imperialists and ensuring national sovereignty on a nationwide scale.

The master of Korea is the Korean people. The Korean people cannot tolerate the foreign imperialists partitioning their territory and trampling upon their national sovereignty. They must restore the lost national sovereignty and become the real master of Korea by ousting the foreign forces and reunifying the country.

In the past our Party, keeping firmly to the Juche position, has tirelessly struggled for national reunification.

The basic policy consistently followed by our Party in the

struggle for national reunification is to attain the goal independently by the Korean people themselves, free from any outside interference, and by peaceful means on the democratic principle. In accordance with this basic policy, and reflecting correctly the requirements of the developments in our country and the wishes of our nation, our Party presented on many occasions the most fair and reasonable proposals for national reunification acceptable to anyone, and exerted every possible effort for their realization.

The south Korean people, too, waged a tenacious struggle for the reunification of our divided country against the U.S. imperialists and their henchmen, thus delivering telling blows to the enemies. Recently, the people from all walks of life in south Korea have fought vigorously demanding the repeal of the fascist "Revitalized Constitution" and the resignation of the traitorous, reactionary "government," in the face of the unprecedentedly intensified brutal suppression of the reactionaries in power. The brave struggles waged incessantly by the south Korean people ever since liberation are righteous patriotic struggles for the democratization of the south Korean society and the hastening of the independent, peaceful reunification of the country.

The correct reunification policy of our Party and the Government of the Republic and the indefatigable struggle of the entire Korean people for its materialization have in recent years brought about some progress in the bid for the solution of the reunification question, but the road to the country's reunification is still beset with great difficulties and obstacles. The internal and external separatists including the U.S. imperialists are not only opposed to the fair reunification proposals of our Party and the Government of the Republic, but also attempting to divide our country into "two Koreas" forever.

The country's reunification is a unanimous, ardent desire of all our nation. Korea must be reunified at all costs, and never be divided into "two Koreas." Our people have lived as a homogeneous nation in the same land for thousands of years. They have one spoken and written language, and their history and cultural traditions are the same. Our country has no national minority. That our people, who have lived as a homogeneous nation in a unified state for ages, should be divided into two in our times, is impermissible either from the viewpoint of the communist ideas or from the standpoint of the nationalist ideas. We must crush by all means the separatists' attempt to create "two Koreas," prevent the permanent division of the nation, and open the doors of reunification as soon as possible.

The country's independent, peaceful reunification requires, first of all, the elimination of foreign interference which is the main barrier to reunification.

The chief outside force that stands in the way of our country's independent, peaceful reunification is U.S. imperialism. U.S. imperialism is the very criminal that occupied south Korea by force of arms and has spelled the pains of national division for our parents, brothers, wives and children to be separated between the north and the south for as long as 30 years, and is the archvillain that is now attempting to divide our country forever with its "two Koreas" policy. In the past period the U.S. imperialists invaded our country, maneuvered to partition our nation and perpetrated all kinds of bestial barbarities under the UN flag.

With a view to achieving the country's independent, peaceful reunification, our Party and the Government of the Republic have struggled tirelessly to remove the cap of "UN force" from the U.S. imperialist army of aggression that occupies south Korea and to get all of them to withdraw. Our just struggle has won positive support and encouragement from the progressive people the world over.

Finding it impossible to justify their army's occupation of south Korea any longer with the help of the UN flag, the U.S. imperialists have recently invented a new trick. They have submitted to the 30th session of the UN General Assembly a "resolution" on the dissolution of the "UN Command." This is no more than a poor farce designed to win public favor and fool the world public opinion and, in fact, remain in south Korea in another cap substituting the cap of "UN force."

The "UN force" in south Korea is precisely U.S. troops and, therefore, the dissolution of the "UN Command" and the withdrawal of the U.S. troops are questions absolutely inseparable from each other. The mere dissolution of the "UN Command" without the withdrawal of the U.S. troops from south Korea is, in fact, of little effect in bringing about the independent, peaceful reunification of our country. The U.S. imperialists should drop their silly trick of fraudulence and withdraw all their troops in south Korea, simultaneously with the dissolution of the "UN Command."

For the independent, peaceful reunification of our country the Armistice Agreement should be replaced by a peace agreement on condition that the U.S. imperialist army of aggression is withdrawn from south Korea.

Being an agreement to suspend hostilities, the Korean Armistice Agreement is not an agreement which completely guarantees peace in Korea. At present our country enjoys no lasting peace but is in a state of temporary ceasefire; it is constantly exposed to the threat of invasion on the part of the U.S. imperialists.

The U.S. imperialists have introduced large quantities of modern weapons of destruction including nuclear weapons and military equipment into south Korea and deployed them near the Military Demarcation Line, and egg the warlike elements in south Korea on to perpetrate military provocations against our Republic every day. Particularly after they had been defeated and driven out of Indochina, the U.S. imperialists declared south Korea a "forward defense zone" of the United States, and are threatening us by speaking out that when a war breaks out in Korea the U.S. forces will intervene on a full scale and open hostilities, and even "will not hesitate to use nuclear weapons."

While behaving like this, the U.S. imperialists are making an outcry about a "threat of invasion from the north." They are noisily speaking that the U.S. troops stay in south Korea to stop the "threat of invasion from the north" and that they cannot withdraw their forces because there is this "threat" even now.

There has never been a "threat of invasion from the north" noisily talked about by the U.S. imperialists and the south Korean authorities, nor does it exist even now. We have more than once made it known clearly that we do not want to "invade the south." It is unequivocally pointed out in the North-South Joint Statement that the north and the south should reunify the country peacefully without resorting to arms. It is an invariable policy of our Party and the Government of the Republic that we will not go to arms on any account as long as the enemy leaves us alone.

We insist that a peace agreement be signed between the Democratic People's Republic of Korea and the United States to eliminate the danger of another war and guarantee a durable peace in Korea.

Concrete measures are needed to remove the state of military confrontation between the north and the south following the conclusion of a DPRK-US peace agreement and the withdrawal of U.S. troops from south Korea.

Before anything else, the armed forces of north and south should be cut drastically. We maintain that the military strength of north and south be reduced to 100,000 or less each. At the same time, the north and the south should stop the arms race and military reinforcement and discontinue the introduction of weapons and war equipment from outside. We must thus create real conditions for maintaining and consolidating peace in our country and for its independent, peaceful reunification.

In order to reunify the country independently and peacefully, a national united front should be formed for the whole country on the principle of great national unity.

Reunifying the country is an undertaking for the good of the whole nation, and a national task feasible only when the whole nation unites efforts and struggles for it in firm unity. The formation of a broad national united front for the whole country on the principle of great national unity is a major guarantee for the country's independent, peaceful reunification.

Everyone who loves the country and the people and wants national reunification must rally under the banner of reunification apart from the differences in ideologies, ideals, social systems and religious beliefs. On no account can these differences be a barrier to unity between the Communists and the nationalists, between people from all walks of life, in their endeavors for the reunification of the country.

In their struggle for reunifying the divided country, the Communists in the north and the south Korean nationalists can quite possibly unite and cooperate. The struggle for reunification is a struggle not between the Communists and the nationalists but between patriots and traitors and between the forces of national independence and the imperialist forces of aggression. Although we, the Communists, and the nationalists in south Korea live under different social systems and differ in ideologies and political views, there can be no contradiction between them as long as the reunification question is concerned. Now when even countries and peoples with differing social systems are fighting in concert for a common goal, why cannot we Communists and south Korean nationalists of one and the same descent and nation join hands in the bid for national reunification?

Just as the Communists and other people of all social sections formed a broad anti-Japanese national united front under the banner of fatherland restoration and made common cause in the anti-Japanese struggle in the past, so the people in the northern half of the Republic and people from all walks of life in south Korea—workers, peasants, youth and students, journalists, religious men and politicians—should now form a national united front on a nationwide scale under the banner of national reunification and come out as one in the solemn struggle for the country's independent, peaceful reunification.

In order to form a broad national united front which covers the whole nation, the north and the south should respect and have faith in each other and endeavor to find common denominators instead of differences.

We do not antagonize the nationalists in south Korea nor do we seek to force our ideology and social system on south Korea.

We are ready to hold negotiations at any time with all political parties including the Democratic Republican Party, social organizations and individual personages in south Korea on the reunification question, and to unite and collaborate with them in the cause of national reunification.

If the south Korean authorities truly wish national union and reunification, they must stop their "anti-communist" clamors against the northern half of the Republic, revoke the "anti-communist law" and desist from suppressing the communists and patriots in south Korea. They must change their "anti-communist" policy to the policy of alliance with communism.

Loudly advocating the so-called "confrontation with the accompaniment of dialogue," "competition with the accompaniment of dialogue" and "coexistence with the accompaniment of dialogue," the south Korean authorities are stirring up feelings of antagonism against the northern half of the Republic. This is an act of treachery to the nation aimed at hampering great national unity and freezing the national division, thus keeping our country divided forever into "two Koreas." Confrontation and competition lead straight to division, while unity and collaboration, to reunification. We maintain that the north and the south must unite, collaborate and be unified rather than going in for confrontation, competition and coexistence.

The institution of a north-south Confederation is the most reasonable way to achieve national union and hasten the independent, peaceful reunification of the country. The north-south Confederation we are proposing purports that while maintaining the present political institutions of the north and the south as they are for the time being, a Supreme National Council is formed with representatives of the Government of the Democratic People's Republic of Korea and the south Korean "Government" to settle matters of common national concern in a coordinated way and conduct external activities as a single state under the one nomenclature of the Confederal Republic of Koryo. This will make it possible to guarantee the coordinated development of our nation in all fields of political, economic, military, cultural and foreign affairs, successfully bring about unity and collaboration between the north and the south, and to hasten the complete reunification of the country.

Being a wise people with a strong sense of independence, lofty patriotism, great capacity for united action and strong fighting will, the Korean people can fully solve their national affairs by themselves.

In firm unity under the banner of national reunification, all the people in north and south Korea will finally smash the maneuvers of the separatists within and without to rig up "two Koreas" and will achieve the historic cause of national reunification by all means after driving out the U.S. imperialist aggressors from our land.

**Talk of the Great Leader
Comrade Kim Il Sung with
Editor-in-Chief of Japanese
Politico-Theoretical
Magazine "Sekai"**
[Excerpt]

March 28, 1976

You asked me to explain the reunification question of Korea at length, so I am going to mention, first of all, a few points about the reunification question of our country.

Because the Korean question is a part of the international affairs in general, the problem of Korean reunification is unthinkable apart from the world's situation.

Since your last visit to our country, the world's situation has undergone a very complex change. Recent years have witnessed a great change in the international situation.

The raw materials, fuel and food crises have become aggravated on the worldwide scale and many capitalist and imperialist countries are in the grip of an economic crisis.

The U.S. imperialists, in particular, are in a serious fuel crisis. Saying that the United States has fuel resources to last only for 30 years to come, the Americans themselves speak out loudly that they should secure new fuel markets, new fuel bases.

U.S. Secretary of State Kissinger cannot be regarded as having spoken for nothing when he openly said that if the Arab nations should use the fuel weapon the United States would resort to real weapons. This we can say is a cry of distress expressed by the imperialists gripped in the vise of a crisis.

As the non-aligned states, the countries of the third world put up an energetic struggle to protect their natural resources, the imperialists are falling into an ever serious economic crisis and find themselves floundering in an economic panic.

The imperialists are now making desperate attempts to wriggle out of the economic crisis.

They are intensifying their maneuvers to split and alienate the non-aligned states, the third world countries from each other, perpetrating overthrowing, subversive activities in all parts of the world.

The United States is using its food weapon against the fuel weapon of the third world countries. Besides, it is producing large quantities of weapons and selling them to other countries at high prices, while supplying weapons to such countries as cannot manufacture them to cause them to feud and antagonize and fight among themselves. Thus, it is now trying to get out of the crisis. This is one of the tactics employed now by the U.S. imperialists in Asia and many other parts of the world.

The United States is ostentatiously holding the signboard of "peace" while stepping up its war preparations secretly.

The U.S. authorities are resorting to the double-faced tactics. On the one hand, they employ the tactics of putting up the signboard of "peace" to fool people while, on the other, working craftily to expand military bases and step up war preparations.

Outwardly, the U.S. imperialists are loud-mouthed about "peace" and "easing of tensions," but, in actual fact, have not waived their wild design for world domination. Strategically, the U.S. imperialists are now preparing for a world war.

They are trying to find a way out from the economic crisis by means of war. Seen from a historical point of view, too, this is how the imperialists used to behave themselves. Whenever they found themselves in an acute economic crisis they sought for a solution in a war. Such maneuvers on the part of the imperialists also let loose the First and Second World Wars.

Just before the Second World War, too, the imperialists concluded "non-aggression treaties" and "neutrality pacts" with other countries under the signboard of "peace." But in the long run, they unleashed the war. No war is started on a prearranged date. The imperialists hasten their war preparations behind the screen of "peace" and start war at any time when the chance arrives.

While stepping up the war preparations, the U.S. imperialists are now scheming to find a solution by splitting the countries of the third world and destroying them one by one.

The Korean question, too, should be studied in the context of such aggressive moves of U.S. imperialism.

The U.S. imperialists are applying to Korea the same artifice of aggression they are employing everywhere in the world. They are scheming to divide our country and continue to hold south Korea in their grip.

In trying to keep south Korea in their grip, the U.S. imperialists aim primarily at tightening their control of Japan. They think that only when they have control over Japan can they treat other countries of Asia as colonies.

The U.S. imperialists want to keep south Korea under their thumb partly because they want to make south Korea their permanent raw material base. It is a fact that they lust for the raw materials in south Korea. Some time ago I found an article in a certain country's magazine which predicted that Korea had huge oil deposits, which might possibly touch off troubles in Korea. It looks like that the U.S. imperialists are craving for the oil resources found in the continental shelves near the Korean peninsula.

To the U.S. imperialists it is also essential to have control over south Korea as a military base. They want to seize the whole of Korea and, further, realize their world domination by using south Korea as their military, strategic base. They want south Korea as a military base to deter the Soviet Union and China and tighten their control of Japan.

After their ignominious defeat in Indochina the U.S. imperialists are further straining the situation in our country, precisely because they want to materialize these aggressive ends. The Korean question is more complex now than when I first met you.

At present the U.S. imperialists are blackmailing us seriously with threats of war. By mobilizing the publications in their service they keep clamoring about a "plan for nine-day operations" or a "plan for five-day operations," and are openly speaking out that they would not hesitate to use even nuclear weapons if a war should break out in Korea some day.

They have already deployed numerous nuclear weapons along the Military Demarcation Line in our country, and recently are carrying out boisterous war exercises every day. Some time ago they went to the length of mobilizing their marines stationed in Okinawa for a vociferous war exercise. If they want the peaceful reunification of Korea, why should they keep holding war exercises noisily? Not we but exactly the U.S. imperialists are obstructing the peaceful reunification of Korea.

The U.S. imperialists do not want Korea's reunification, and neither do south Korea's present rulers. The latter are colluding with the former.

The present south Korean rulers are acting strictly on orders from the U.S. Central Intelligence Agency. Therefore, unless they are out of its control, the question cannot be solved. The present rulers of south Korea have handed south Korea over to the U.S. imperialists as a military base and the latter try to continue to use it is a colonial and military base.

Since the U.S. imperialists' strategy to keep Korea divided and perpetuate their occupation of south Korea remains unchanged, we cannot expect their immediate withdrawal from there. In the light of the prevailing situation now, the U.S. imperialists are hardly likely to give up south Korea and withdraw.

The Korean question is confronted with a very great difficulty. So it is by no means a simple matter. The Korean question is more complicated and difficult than the question of Indochina.

In order to drive the U.S. imperialists out of south Korea, the south Korean, Japanese and other Asian peoples must be awakened and fight forcefully against them.

However, the south Korean people and a considerable number of Asian people are not yet sufficiently awakened to the sinister aggressive activities of the U.S. imperialists and they do not wage a vigorous struggle against their presence in Asia and their domination and control of Asian nations. Some south Koreans do hate U.S. imperialism, but there are still some others who regard U.S. imperialism as "benefactor" who gives them some sort of "favor" and think that only when they cling to the U.S. can they be given rice to eat.

The present rulers of south Korea and Japan do not oppose the colonial rule of U.S. imperialism; they obey it faithfully. With its backing, they are craftily working to prevent the peoples from awakening, while harassing and repressing them in various ways. The rulers are engrossing the peoples in finding a way out of their dire poverty.

Judging from the prevailing situation, it seems that the question of Korea's reunification will be solved through a hard-fought struggle.

Now I will reply to your question concerning the situation following the publication of the North-South Joint Statement.

The North-South Joint Statement published in July 1972 makes clear the three principles of national reunification—reunifying the country independently and peacefully and achieving great national unity by transcending the differences in ideologies, ideals and systems. These are good principles.

The three principles clarified in the North-South Joint Statement were proposed by us and the south Korean authorities agreed to them. When publishing this statement, they consented to the three principles—independence, peaceful reunification and great national unity—and solemnly pledged before the whole nation that they would implement them in good faith.

However, as soon as the North-South Joint Statement was published, the south Korean authorities negated one by one the principles and agreements in this statement. They published the North-South Joint Statement on the one hand, and, on the other, negated it. This appears to be the tactics of the U.S. imperialists.

When publishing the North-South Joint Statement, we put forward the principles of independence, presupposing that Koreans should reunify the country by themselves without relying on the U.S. or on any other nations. The south Korean authorities, too, declared that they, as Koreans, would seek a policy of national reunification for themselves, without relying on a great power or any other foreign countries.

But at a press conference held the day after the publication of the North-South Joint Statement, a high-ranking official of south Korea made an absurd statement that because the UN was not an outside force, the "UN forces" must continue to be stationed in south Korea. This was a plain utterance that rejected the principle of independence made clear in the North-South Joint Statement. If, when meeting us, the south Korean authorities had said that they tried to solve the question of national reunification through relying on outside forces or they intended to perpetuate the division of the country, we would never have published the Joint Statement with them.

The south Korean authorities also denied the principle of great national unity agreed upon in the North-South Joint Statement. If the south Korean authorities had even the slightest willingness to collaborate with us on the principle of great national unity, transcending the differences in ideologies, ideals and systems, they should desist from their anti-communist policy. How can they achieve the great national unity, opposing communism, instead of collaborating with communists? Following the publication of the North-South Joint Statement, the south Korean authorities intensified their "anti-communist" campaign, slandering and opposing the northern half of the Republic; they claimed that there was no reason, no ground whatsoever for them to revise the "anti-communist law" and the "national security law."

The puppet clique of south Korea continued with their activities for national partition in violation of the principles and agreements of the North-South Joint Statement on the independent and peaceful reunification of the country and, in June 1973, they advocated that the north and south of our country should enter the UN separately. This laid bare their true intention to internationally legalize and perpetuate our nation's division. Since liberation up to date our people have already suffered indescribably great misfortunes and pains because of the split of the territory and nation, and how can we tolerate their activities to perpetuate it? As the U.S. imperialists do not quit south Korea, it is impossible to reunify the country right away, but it is absolutely unnecessary to legalize the division. We cannot legalize and recognize the permanent division of the country.

Legalizing and perpetuating the division of the nation is a treachery to sell out the country and the people, it is a crime that can never be erased out of history. We have no desire at all to hand down to posterity a historical record of treachery on the country and the nation being sold out.

Why, then, is the north-south dialogue at a stalemate now?

At present the south Korean authorities are alleging that the north-south dialogue has been disrupted because we are insincere. But that is not true.

We started the north-south dialogue for the purpose of creating favorable conditions for achieving great national unity and hastening the country's reunification as much as practicable. In order to achieve the great national unity in accordance with the principles of the North-South Joint Statement, it is necessary to guarantee the democratization of society and the freedom of political activity of all political parties, groupings and personages of all walks of life.

The south Korean authorities, however, are imprisoning and savagely repressing many patriotic democrats, youth and students of south Korea who fight against the division of the country and for the democratization of south Korean society. The reactionary rulers of south Korea had Kim Dae Jung kidnapped in Japan in broad daylight and are repressing him through a trial, because he opposed their treacherous policies against the country and the people; and they jailed poet Kim Ji Ha because he had written a poem that criticized them. They stigmatize any opponent as a communist and, on the charge of the violation of the "anti-communist law," arrest, imprison and murder brutally. The reactionary south Korean rulers are repressing numerous religious people and even the former south Korean "President" Yun Bo Son

224   KIM IL SUNG

on the charge of the violation of the "anti-communist law."
Nobody would believe that such people as the religious people and
Yun Bo Son are communists.

How can we meet the south Korean authorities and hold a
dialogue when they are repressing the patriotic democrats, youth
and students so harshly? We can no longer tolerate the fact that
the south Korean authorities are intensifying their repression of
south Korea's patriotic democrats, youth and students behind the
signboard of dialogue.

And since the south Korean authorities are trying to continue to
keep foreign forces and working to perpetuate the division of the
country, we cannot resume our dialogue with them. We mean to
have talks in order to reunify the country; and what is the use of
meeting them when the south Korean authorities try to keep the
country divided? It is of no use to hold talks for the partition of the
country with those who seek the division of the country.

In the present situation the resumption of the north-south
dialogue is impossible, however hard we try to resume it. The
present south Korean authorities do not understand our intentions, because they have no policy, think nothing of the nation and
humanity, and have no logic. A dialogue is tenable when each
party's intentions are understood, so how can a dialogue be held
when we are not understood?

We can resume the dialogue even now if the south Korean
authorities stop repressing the democrats, release the arrested
and detained youth, students and patriots, desist from their fascist
rule and take the road to democracy, stop the activities for national
division and move toward reunification.

We have never disrupted the north-south dialogue; we always
keep the door open to the dialogue. We have proposed on a
number of occasions to convoke a Great National Congress
composed of representatives of all political parties and social
organizations, personages of various circles and the democratic
republican party of south Korea included, and hold discussions on
problems of the reunification of the nation.

Next, I will answer to your question on the peace agreement.

Right now, our country is in frontal confrontation with the U.S.

imperialists. So we must conclude a peace agreement with the U.S.; we cannot do so with anybody else.

It is the U.S. imperialist aggressors who are acting as masters in south Korea now. They have full command of armed forces there. It is also the U.S. imperialists who concluded the Military Armistice Agreement with us. The question of replacing the Armistice Agreement with a peace agreement should be settled only by the Democratic People's Republic of Korea and the U.S. authorities, that actually signed the Armistice Agreement and have real powers to guarantee peace in Korea.

The south Korean authorities oppose our reasonable proposal; they ask how it is possible to have U.S. troops withdrawn from south Korea and conclude a peace agreement without any alternative. But we have made clear the detailed measures to be taken after the conclusion of the peace agreement.

As one of the detailed measures for easing tensions between north and south after the signing of the Korea-US peace agreement on condition that U.S. troops are withdrawn from south Korea, we proposed, first of all, to reduce the number of the armed forces of the north and the south to 100,000 or less respectively. In addition, we proposed that the north and south prevent armed conflict with each other and refrain from resorting to force of arms against each other and that both parties resume talks on the country's reunification in accordance with the three principles of national reunification clarified in the North-South Joint Statement. It is absolutely untrue that we have no specific proposal as to what is to be done following the conclusion of the peace agreement.

Although the specific steps to be taken after the conclusion of the peace agreement between Korea and the U.S. were explained, the U.S. and south Korean authorities deliberately claim that we have no specific plans because they do not want to conclude a peace agreement. The U.S. authorities are unwilling to sign a peace agreement with us.

Two years have elapsed since a letter was sent to the United States Congress in the name of the Supreme People's Assembly of the Democratic People's Republic of Korea, proposing that negotiations be held on the question of replacing the Korean Armistice Agreement with a peace agreement. But the United States has not yet replied to the letter. And last year the UN

General Assembly adopted a resolution calling on the signatory powers to the Military Armistice Agreement of Korea to withdraw the U.S. troops from south Korea and replace the Armistice Agreement with a peace agreement. The U.S. imperialists are ignoring the resolution of the UN General Assembly as well. Even a UN General Assembly resolution falls flat with the U.S. imperialists. To the U.S. imperialists only what they themselves utter makes law but what others say cannot be law. This is just what the U.S. imperialists are like.

Judging by all the facts, the United States authorities do not want to conclude a peace agreement with us because they aim to prevent the reunification of our country and keep it divided forever.

When we proposed to the United States to conclude a peace agreement, the south Korean authorities came forward with a proposal for the so-called "non-aggression treaty." This "treaty" is not designed for the reunification of our country. The purpose of the "treaty" is that the north and the south of Korea should remain divided as two states and promise not to attack each other. In the final analysis, this is designed to legalize the partition of our country. Even though our country is divided temporarily, why should we sign a meaningless "non-aggression treaty" legalizing the division? The peace agreement we proposed and the "non-aggression treaty" the south Korean authorities put forward are essentially different.

The U.S. imperialists and the south Korean authorities keep on fussing about the fictitious "threat of southward invasion." In Korea today there exists the threat of northward invasion from the south, not the "threat of southward invasion" from the north. Not we but precisely the U.S. imperialists and the south Korean authorities are creating the danger of war; we are not threatening south Korea but the U.S. imperialists are threatening us. Who will believe that such a small country as ours is threatening the United States which is seeking to dominate the world? Nobody in the world would believe it. And yet the U.S. imperialists and the south Korean authorities persist in their unfounded argument that we are threatening south Korea. Quite contrary is the fact; the

Americans are threatening us, refusing to conclude a peace agreement and hold a dialogue with us.

What, then, should be done in the future to solve the question of Korea's reunification?

In my opinion there must be some conditions matured and a certain length of time needed for the realization of Korea's reunification. The people's struggle will never emerge victorious automatically.

The reunification of our country requires, first of all, the awakening of both the south Korean people and the Japanese people.

The people in south Korea and the Japanese people should awaken and wage a joint struggle against U.S. imperialist aggression and interference, thus making it impossible for the U.S. imperialists to control south Korea and Japan any longer. This is prerequisite to an early solution of the question of our country's reunification. But as yet their forces are not strong enough to do so.

The democratic forces in south Korea are now fighting in difficult conditions caused by the south Korean puppets' repression which is being intensified under the U.S. imperialists' wirepulling. But I think the south Korean and Japanese peoples will be further awakened through their struggle in the future, since they suffered greatly in the past and waged many struggles to extricate themselves from the sufferings.

Although they are now living helplessly, the south Korean people will certainly become awakened under the enemy's intensified fascist repression and gradually turn out in a struggle. Historical experience affords good illustrations of this.

The more cruel the reactionaries' repression becomes, the more the people will be awakened.

Broad sections of the people in the world are now gradually awakening in the course of struggle. Thus the general situation is developing in favor of world peace and the progressive people the world over.

A few days ago I met a Government Friendship Delegation from Ethiopia. In monarchical Ethiopia the reactionary rulers suppressed the people very cruelly. The rulers' suppression of the people reached the extremes and the people suffered from starvation. Thus the people's anti-government sentiments mounted daily and, at last, young officers rose in revolt and toppled the monarchical regime. After the overthrow of monarchism Ethiopia is following the progressive path. At present Ethiopia is carrying out land reform and making a national democratic revolution in many respects.

The state of affairs in Portugal is similar. In the past Portugal was no less fascistized than Spain under Franco's reign. But now the people are striving energetically to follow the road of democratic development. Of course, that country has a number of complicated problems yet to be solved. But, in any case, the more ruthlessly the people are suppressed, the more rapidly the progressive forces grow. This has been proved by facts.

The democratic forces of south Korea are weak now, but the south Korean people will sooner or later awaken to become a formidable force for national reunification. The south Korean people can never go in rags and hungry indefinitely without any political liberties and rights, under the oppression of the puppet clique.

I believe many of the Japanese people think that Japan should get out of U.S. control and follow the path of independence.

Further, it is of importance for the solution of Korea's reunification question to arouse more extensively the world public opinion subscribing to the reunification of Korea and expose before the people throughout the world the unwarranted acts committed by the U.S. imperialists in south Korea.

It is necessary to arouse the opinion of the peoples of the world on the Korean question on a wider scale, so that broader segments of the peoples of the world should be acquainted better with the national misery and distress the Korean people are suffering owing to the division of the country and the nation.

Now the south Korean authorities are scheming to fascistize south Korea as the Franco clique of Spain did, but it is no more than a fantastic daydream.

In the future, we will widely introduce and publicize to the peoples of the world the criminal barbarities perpetrated by the U.S. imperialists in south Korea and the pains suffered by the south Korean people under the fascist tyranny, and more vigorously stir up the world public opinion on the Korean question. At present the opinion of the peoples of the world as to the goings-on in south Korea is not called up as widely as it should be.

Only when the opinion of the peoples throughout the world supporting the Korean people's cause of reunification is aroused more briskly, is it possible to avert war in Korea, preserve peace in Asia and reunify Korea in a peaceful way. We will strive to arouse world public opinion on the Korean question more vigorously and thus make the Korean question the focal point of attention both in Asian and world affairs.

When the opinion of the peoples of the world regarding the Korean question is stirred up, the awareness of the people and democrats in south Korea will also increase and their fighting will and spirit rise higher. In particular, when the solidarity movement is conducted briskly in Japan in support of the Korean people's struggle for national reunification, it will further stimulate the south Korean people in their democratic movement.

Now, on your question concerning our foreign policy.

Our foreign policy is the same as in the past.

The important aspect of our foreign policy is to strengthen solidarity with the third world countries, the non-aligned countries.

Since their latest economic crisis started, the U.S. imperialists have intensified their activities to split the third world countries and the non-aligned countries. In disuniting these countries, they try to take advantage of their vulnerable points. As for those countries that are short of food, the U.S. imperialists give them some food in an effort to realize their demands; and they provide some countries with weapons in order to make their political demands on them. On the whole, the present U.S. imperialist strategy is to disorganize the third world countries and the non-aligned countries to prevent them from uniting together.

The U.S. imperialists fear the unity of the third world countries more than anything else. Through their experience at the UN the U.S. imperialists have often felt that the unity of the third world countries is undesirable. As the third world countries united and vigorously fought to prevent the reduction of the prices of raw materials and against their arbitrary plunder, the U.S. imperialists were more terror-stricken. So the U.S. imperialists are now stretching out their hands not only to Latin American countries but also to Asian and African countries, and are carrying out extensive activities to divide these countries.

Our present policy is to do all we can to prevent the third world countries from being disunited and strengthen their solidarity.

At present the third world countries have quite a few hardships. First of all, they have many economic bottlenecks. Therefore, it is essential for the third world countries to strengthen their economic cooperation. The third world countries can overcome the economic difficulties if they closely cooperate with each other on the principle of filling each other's needs.

The next headache for the third world countries is that they have not yet solved the question of their own native cadres. In the past when they ruled these countries, the imperialists prevented them from training the native cadres. As a result, these countries have now very few technicians: all they have are only some experts of civic science.

At present the third world countries are laying emphasis on agriculture, which I think is very good.

In recent years, under the influence of the cold front, not only the countries situated north of the equator but also those near it have suffered great damages. In this situation, it is very important that the third world countries take agriculture in hand, determined to solve the food problem for themselves. Taking agriculture in hand will enable them to solve the food problem for their peoples quickly and thus preserve their national independence and sovereignty.

Our country is increasing economic cooperation and political unity with the third world countries, the non-aligned countries. It is true that ours is a small country, and we cannot give much help to other countries economically. However, we pass on our experience to the third world countries and send them our technicians who are capable of undertaking irrigation projects.

With the Summit Conference of Non-Aligned States ahead, the non-aligned countries are making preparations to take part in the conference. Now everybody consents to the non-aligned countries forging unity. But what is important is how the non-aligned countries should achieve their unity and how they can avoid playing into the hands of the imperialists. Therefore, I think, the forthcoming Summit Conference of Non-Aligned States will extensively discuss the strengthening of their international solidarity.

The third world countries will not be disorganized and cut into pieces in accordance with the imperialist strategy. The people are sharply watching the maneuvers of the imperialists. The U.S. CIA will not be able to pull the wool over the eyes of the people no matter what crafty and insidious artifice it may resort to. The wild ambition of the U.S. imperialists will be frustrated in the long run.

These are my general answers. If you have any further questions you may ask.

Question: May I understand that there still remain unchanged your conceptions of the spirit of the July 4 North-South Joint Statement, the proposals made by your country after its publication, in particular, on the Confederal Republic of Koryo advanced on June 23, 1973 by Your Excellency Mr. President?

Answer: Our proposals made in the North-South Joint Statement are still effective. We intend to make continued efforts to carry our point.

However, we do not mean that we will never agree to other than what we propose. If both the north and south sit together and have serious discussions, there may emerge better proposals. Then we are ready to agree to them. Even if some of our views are not accepted, we will not insist only on our views for the sake of great national unity and the country's reunification. We are going to subordinate everything to great national unity and to the cause of national reunification.

Question: Your Excellency Mr. President always says that you will not interfere with south Korea, that you have no intention to impose the socialist system on south Korea, and that different political systems can exist and people with different religious beliefs can live in one country. Nevertheless, there have been various speculations about this. What are your views?

Answer: At present the south Korean rulers are spreading a lie that we intend to "communize" south Korea and impose communism on it. More than once we have already declared that we would not force socialism upon south Korea. If we do not impose the socialist system of the northern half of the Republic on south Korea and the south Korean authorities do not try to destroy our socialist system, we think, we, both of us, as one and the same nation, can move forward together while keeping two systems intact. If both sides settle problems of common national interest and concern by united efforts, it will be greatly conducive to the coordinated progress of the country and the people.

True, class antagonisms have already disappeared in the northern half of the Republic, but the class problem is yet to be solved in south Korea. How to settle class relations in south Korea is a matter of the south Korean people themselves. We will not meddle in it.

Question: Those who well understand what Your Excellency Mr. President has just said interpret it correctly. But some people, while gradually forming correct views through struggles, are apprehensive lest socialism should be imposed on them amid possible confusion after they have overthrown Pak Jung Hi through hard efforts. What are your views on this?

Answer: At present some south Korean democrats fear lest the communists might take advantage of their democratic movement to impose socialism on them. We have more than once declared that we will not impose socialism on south Korea. So we will not do such a thing.

Let the south Korean people themselves choose the road to take. If socialism is forced on them, they will suffer indigestion. It is meaningless to force socialism on those who do not understand socialism correctly.

We have no intention to impose socialism on south Korea; and we have no plan to do so. In dealing with any question we are consistent in our opposition to subjectivism. Subjectivism is incompatible with the principle of socialism and communism.

Question: At present the U.S. has nuclear warheads in south Korea. And last year the U.S. Secretary of State threatened and blackmailed your country, declaring that if you "invade the south" they would check it with nuclear weapons. As regards this statement, I would like to ask Your Excellency Mr. President if you have the idea of forestalling it with nuclear weapons.

Answer: We have no intention of arming ourselves with nuclear weapons. We have not enough money to produce nuclear weapons or any adequate place to test them.

The U.S. imperialists say they will use nuclear weapons if war breaks out in Korea, in order to browbeat us.

Even if war bursts forth in Korea, they would not be able to use nuclear weapons. How can they use nuclear weapons here in Korea when the opposing forces will grapple with each other? Should the enemy use nuclear weapons, he will also get killed. That is why I called fools those who said they would use nuclear weapons if war broke out in Korea.

At present the south Korean rulers are stubbornly asking the U.S. imperialists for a nuclear umbrella, but we do not ask other countries for nuclear weapons or a nuclear umbrella.

Question: The speculation is rife concerning negotiations between your country and the U.S. I would like to hear Your Excellency Mr. President's views on it.

Answer: We have a lot of problems, including that of a peace agreement, on which we must settle an account with the U.S. authorities. So we do not mean that we are not willing to have any talks or contact with them.

But under any circumstances, we will have talks or contact with the U.S. on an equal footing, not in such a way as to entreat them.

We are ready to have talks with the U.S. authorities even now if they accept our proposal to replace the Armistice Agreement with a peace agreement. But the U.S. authorities have not yet given any answer to our proposal on the conclusion of a peace agreement or have shown any affirmative reaction. Therefore, we do not want to go to the trouble of knocking at the door, begging them for a dialogue.

We have already tapped at the door, asking the U.S. for talks on the question of concluding a peace agreement. But the U.S. authorities have given us no reply. So, we cannot ask them to have talks with us against their will, can we?

Question: There has recently been much talk about "cross recognition." I know well that Your Excellency Mr. President is totally against it. If China, the Soviet Union, the United States and Japan take some initiatives, and this not in the form of "cross recognition," in connection with the reunification of your country, will you reject all of them no matter what they are?

Answer: The question of other countries' so-called "cross recognition" of the north and the south of our country is also connected with the fundamental question of the reunification of the country.

The present "government" of south Korea is against national reunification, insists on the split of the nation, keeps the outside forces by the sleeve and hinders great national unity. So, the recognition of this "government" implies not reunification but permanent division for our country. The south Korean authorities prattle that reunification would be possible even after the north and the south join the UN as "two Koreas." This is a hackneyed trick of the quislings. We can never agree to the so-called "cross recognition" proposed by the U.S. imperialists and their lackeys for the purpose of creating "two Koreas" and dividing our country into north and south for good.

Some people say: the present south Korean authorities hold reins of "government," and how can they be ignored? But the present "government" of south Korea is not an independent government the independent states should deal with. Therefore, as far as this "government" exists there can be no "cross recognition" of the north and the south of our country.

We are positively opposed not only to the question of "cross recognition" of the north and the south of Korea, but also to any form of initiatives that envisage the division of our nation. Of course, as far as an initiative leading to our country's reunification is concerned, that is another matter.

As for the present south Korean "government," no relations should be maintained with it, but it must be thoroughly isolated. Positive support should be given to the people of south Korea in their struggle for democracy, so that a democratic government is established in south Korea. If the south Korean authorities stop fascist suppression—arresting and jailing people and democrats—and if they frankly admit their past crimes against the country and the people and promise to stop such acts, then the matter will be different.

**Talk with Pakistani
Journalists** [Excerpt]

May 27, 1976

N ow, I will answer your question about the reunification of
Korea.

To reunify the divided country is the greatest desire of the
Korean people and one of the most important struggle goals of the
Government of our Republic.

Ever since the division of the country into the north and the
south we have exerted every effort to reunify it. We advanced the
basic policy that the country's reunification should be achieved
without any foreign interference, independently by the Korean
people themselves, on a democratic basis and through peaceful
means, and put forth many specific proposals to carry this policy
into effect.

However, none of our reasonable proposals for reunification was
materialized on account of the insincere attitudes taken by the
south Korean authorities and the U.S. side.

As you know, in 1972 a joint statement of the north and south
was made public. The statement elucidated the three principles for

the country's reunification. These three principles I myself advanced when representatives of the south Korean side came to Pyongyang.

The content of the three principles is: First, to realize the reunification independently without reliance on or interference by foreign forces; second, to achieve the reunification peacefully without recourse to force of arms by the north and the south; and third, to achieve great national unity, transcending differences in ideologies, ideals and systems.

The south Korean authorities accepted the three principles, considering them reasonable. But they completely trampled down the spirit of the north-south joint statement on the day after its publication, even before its ink dried.

They claimed that the "UN forces" in south Korea could not be regarded as a foreign force. And saying that there was no need to amend the "anti-communist law," an obstacle to great national unity, the south Korean authorities kept up their "anti-communist" racket, repressing and murdering south Korean democrats and patriots right and left.

Nevertheless, we made all our sincere efforts to keep the spirit of the three principles prevailing by all means and solve the question of national reunification peacefully through negotiations between the north and the south.

The south Korean authorities did not want the reunification of the country from the outset. They dragged on the north-south talks, advocating the "confrontation," "competition" and "coexistence" of the north and south in the state of being divided.

We hold that the north and south should not confront each other but unite, should not compete but cooperate, should not coexist but reunite.

The south Korean authorities went so far as to propose separate UN membership of the north and south, with our country kept divided.

We are categorically opposed to our country's entry into the UN as "two Koreas." As also mentioned by His Excellency Mr. Prime Minister Bhutto this time, if our country is admitted to the UN as "two Koreas," it will keep our nation divided into two for ever and legalize Korea's partition internationally. No single nation will ever want to see itself divided into two for good. And it goes without saying that our people, who have been suffering from the misfortune and pains of national division over three decades, cannot tolerate a permanent national division.

We proposed to institute a north-south confederation to prevent a permanent national division and accelerate the reunification of the country. We claim to form a supreme national congress with representatives of the DPRK and the south Korean authorities, leaving intact the present political systems in the north and south for the time being, to solve the questions of common interest for the nation, to go externally as one state under the single name of Confederal Republic, and to enter the UN as a single state representing the whole nation of Korea.

You asked if it is high time for the north and south to institute a confederation. We think it is long overdue. True, the north-south confederation has not yet been realized because of foreign interference and the obstructionist moves of the partitionists at home and abroad. We believe, however, that our aspirations will be definitively met by the just struggle of the entire people of north and south Korea. They will join efforts and shatter the interference of all outside forces and certainly reunify their divided country before long.

You asked whether it is true that we will not impose a socialist system on south Korea. I have already spoken on this point many times. I did in a number of my interviews with foreign journalists, and on every opportunity.

For the sake of the great unity of the whole nation we will not impose a socialist system on south Korea; we have no such intention at all. What kind of social system should be set up in south Korea, it is a matter for the south Korean people to decide.

As to the point on the north and south refraining from forcing their social systems on each other it is clearly expounded in the third of the three principles for national reunification laid down in the north-south joint statement. It points out that great national unity should be promoted transcending the differences in ideologies, ideals and systems. We want to live together, with the north and south not imposing their ideologies, ideals, systems or religious beliefs on each other, in accordance with the principle of great national unity.

We consider that the two different systems in the north and the south will provide no ground precluding the great unity of the entire nation.

The allegation that we are going to impose the socialist system upon south Korea is a nonsense uttered by the secessionists to obstruct the great unity of our nation and Korea's reunification.

It is very important to strictly adhere to the principle of great national unity in order to prevent our nation's permanent division into two and attain national reunification. We will do our best to realize the great unity of the whole nation and achieve the country's independent, peaceful reunification.

Now I would answer your question regarding the establishment of a new international economic order by the developing countries.

The old international economic order was set up by the imperialists and colonialists in the past; it is an order aimed at exploiting the oppressed nations and the peoples of the colonial countries.

Many countries of the world have now attained independence. It is true that there are still countries that are fighting for national liberation, but many of those Asian, African and Latin American countries which were former colonies have won national liberation and embarked upon the building of a new life.

However, the old international economic order set up by the imperialists and colonialists still remains in existence. This order greatly hampers the newly-independent countries in their efforts to defend their sovereignty and national independence and build an independent national economy.

The peoples of all countries of the world must unite firmly and fight to abolish the old international economic order set up by the imperialists.

At present the imperialists and colonialists are indulging in all kinds of plots and moves of estrangement, disruption and subversion in order to undermine the solidarity of the peoples of the third world, peoples of the developing countries. Thus, the imperialists, doing everything to prevent the developing countries from uniting and blasting the old international economic order, are trying to maintain this order.

Under these circumstances, it is necessary, above all, for the peoples of the third world, peoples of the developing countries to strengthen their solidarity in order to scrap the old international economic order and establish a new one. The peoples of the developing countries should cement unity and thus lay bare and smash the subversive activities of the imperialists and colonialists.

It is our belief that if the peoples of the third world countries struggle in firm unity, they will be able to destroy the old international economic order and establish a new one. At present the peoples of many countries express a firm resolve to blast the old international economic order once and for all by strengthening the solidarity of the peoples of the third world with a fresh courage and fighting spirit in order to build an independent national economy and consolidate national sovereignty and independence.

We think that without fighting and without uniting their strength the developing countries will not be able to receive a "gift" of a new international economic order from the imperialists and colonialists.

Further, you asked about the question of establishing a nuclear-free zone in south Asia and the Middle East. We are of the opinion that the struggle of the peoples in these areas for a nuclear-free zone in south Asia and the Middle East is just.

We think that the nuclear danger should be eliminated and a stable peace and security ensured not only in these areas but also in all other parts of the world. We demand that in order to free all parts of the world from nuclear danger all nuclear weapons be scrapped.

You asked me about my opinion of the Summit Conference of Non-Aligned Countries to be held in Colombo. Now I would like to make a brief remark.

As you know, our country joined the non-aligned states at their foreign ministers' conference in Lima last year. So, I think our government delegation should participate in the Colombo Summit without fail.

We devote great attention to the Colombo Summit. The non-alignment movement now comprises more than 80 countries, and this is a very great force. Our delegation will bend every effort and energy to make the Summit Conference of the Non-Aligned Countries a historic conference.

The agenda-items of the Colombo Summit are under discussion as yet.

In our opinion, it should take up, above all, the question of how to assess the current international situation, and a number of economic problems including the issue of international economic development. In particular, it should discuss measures to oppose the old international economic order set up by the imperialists in pursuance of their economic interests and establish a new one in the interests of the progressive people of the world.

It also should discuss measures to curb the moves of the imperialists towards division, subversion, estrangement and bribery and to strengthen the unity of the new-born independent countries, the non-aligned countries, and the problem of supporting and encouraging the struggles of peoples for freedom and independence, and national prosperity.

Our government delegation will attend the forthcoming summit of the non-aligned countries and bend every effort to make it a great success by actively contributing to the discussion of all questions, including the questions of further strengthening unity and economic and technical cooperation among the non-aligned states and supporting and encouraging the people's struggle for national liberation and independence.

You asked me about my view on the liberation struggle of the southern African peoples. Now I would make a brief remark.

In the past period the peoples of the African Continent have waged a vigorous struggle for freedom and independence.

Thanks to the unyielding struggle of the African peoples and the active support and encouragement of the peace-loving people throughout the world, many African countries have won national independence and freedom and attained a great victory in their struggle against colonialism.

But some countries in southern Africa have not yet achieved complete liberation. The peoples of Zimbabwe, Namibia and Azania continue to fight courageously, weapons in hand, against colonialism and racism.

The colonialists and racists are now trying in every way to check the liberation struggle of the peoples in this region. But the liberation struggle of the southern African peoples, like the struggle of the peoples in other parts of the African Continent, will surely triumph, and the colonialists and racists will finally meet their doom on the African Continent.

The Korean and Pakistani peoples will, in the future too, as in the past, give active support to the African peoples in their revolutionary struggle for national liberation and independence. This was reaffirmed in the recent talks between His Excellency Mr. Prime Minister Bhutto and us, and is reflected in the joint communique, too.

Lastly, I will briefly answer your question about the change that has taken place in the world arena since my meeting with Mr. Prime Minister Zulfikar Ali Bhutto in Djakarta ten years ago.

In the past ten years great changes have taken place in the international arena.

First of all, a fundamental change has taken place in the balance of forces. The peoples of the world have won a great victory in the struggle against imperialism and colonialism, whereas the imperialist forces have weakened greatly.

The might of the socialist countries has further increased and many countries of the world are advancing towards socialism.

Under the banner of anti-imperialism and independence many countries of Asia, Africa and Latin America have cast off the colonial yoke of imperialism and won independence, and entered on the road of creating a new life. The new-emerging forces, the great anti-imperialist revolutionary forces of our times, have emerged amidst the flames of the national-liberation struggle.

The imperialists are encountering a strong resistance of the peoples in all parts and all countries of the world.

A special mention should be made of the fact that the imperialists are now facing a grave economic crisis. The capitalist and imperialist countries are going through acute fuel and raw material crises. Of late, the countries of the third world, the developing countries, have stepped up the struggle to defend their political sovereignty and achieve economic independence. This has further aggravated the economic crisis in the imperialist countries.

Generally speaking, the international situation in the past ten years has developed in favor of the progressive peoples of the world, the peoples of the third world, to the disadvantage of the imperialists, and on the international arena the anti-imperialist, revolutionary forces have grown in strength from day to day, whereas the imperialist forces of aggression have declined and become weaker.

The present times can be called the times of independence when all peoples of the world demand independence and sovereignty. No country and no nation want to be subjected to others and will tolerate their independence being trampled underfoot.

The once exploited and oppressed peoples have appeared on the world stage as the masters exercising their rights; the voices demanding independence are rising higher every day and the struggle to defend independence is further strengthened on the international scene.

In order to get out of their catastrophic economic crisis and oppress and exploit the peoples of the newly-independent countries, the imperialists are now resorting to ever more crafty methods. They are strengthening the moves to disunite the nations of the newly-emerging forces and, by means of double-dealing tactics, are deceiving people under the signboard of "peace" on the one hand and, on the other, stepping up war preparations.

However, if the peoples of the third world and newly-independent countries and all the progressive peoples of the world, united more firmly, see through the imperialists' crafty double-dealing tactics and wage a vigorous struggle against it, they can successfully frustrate the imperialists' artifice no matter how crafty.

Such, in general, is the change that has taken place in the international arena since I met His Excellency Mr. Prime Minister Zulfikar Ali Bhutto ten years ago, and the present international situation.

I am confident that as in the past, so in the future, the Governments and peoples of Korea and Pakistan will vigorously wage a joint struggle against imperialism and colonialism in unity with the peace-loving people of the world and the third world peoples, under the unfurled banner of anti-imperialism and independence and, by so doing, surely win victory in their efforts to build a new, peaceful and prosperous society.

Answer to a Question put by the Foreign Editor of the Yugoslav news agency Tanjug

May 29, 1976

Question: What methods can the non-aligned countries employ to support the reunification of Korea?

ANSWER: The question of the Korean reunification, as a question of restoring the territory and people robbed by the foreign imperialists and establishing the sovereignty of the Korean nation for the whole country, is a link in the common cause of the non-aligned countries against imperialism and for independence. Therefore, in order to achieve the reunification of Korea it is necessary to strengthen the unity with the international revolutionary forces while increasing our own internal revolutionary forces.

The Korean people have always enjoyed support and encouragement from the non-aligned countries in their struggle to make the U.S. army withdraw from south Korea and achieve the independent, peaceful reunification of the country. The Heads of State of many non-aligned countries have until now actively supported our people's cause of national reunification in the international arena, including the Summit Conferences of Non-Aligned Countries. Particularly the Fourth Summit denounced the foreign interference in the internal affairs of Korea and the "two Koreas" plot, and adopted a resolution demanding the withdrawal of all foreign troops occupying south Korea under the UN flag.

This support and encouragement of the non-aligned countries greatly inspire our people in their struggle for the independent, peaceful reunification of the country.

The first question which must be solved for the independent, peaceful reunification of Korea is the withdrawal of all foreign troops from south Korea and the replacement of the Korean Armistice Agreement with a peace agreement, in accordance with the resolution of the 30th session of the UN General Assembly. In solving such questions, our people highly value the active support and encouragement of the non-aligned countries.

Today an important question facing the non-aligned countries in supporting the Korean people's struggle for national reunification is to make south Korea too hot for the U.S. imperialists by more extensively arousing world public opinion supporting the reunification of Korea. This is essential to prevent another war in Korea, preserve peace in Asia and the rest of the world, and reunify Korea independently by peaceful means. We hope that the non-aligned countries will thoroughly isolate U.S. imperialism and the south Korean puppet clique in all parts of the world and widely expose their criminal moves for another war in south Korea and their "two Koreas" plot, thus more strongly arousing world public opinion supporting the independent, peaceful reunification of Korea.

It is our firm belief that the non-aligned countries will, in the future, too, as in the past, express active support and firm solidarity for the Korean people's struggle for the independent, peaceful reunification of the country and take positive measures helpful to Korea's reunification at the forthcoming Fifth Summit in particular.

I take this opportunity to express my deep thanks to the governments and peoples of the non-aligned countries including Yugoslavia for the active support and encouragement they have rendered so far to the Korean people in their cause of independent, peaceful reunification.